Strength Thro

Cory Mathews

Ephesians 6:12 Publishing

Strength Through The Struggle

Published by Ephesians 612 Publishing |
www.ephesians612publishing.com
For information about special discounts for bulk purchases, please contact
Ephesians 612 Publishing special sales department at
info@ephesians612publishing.com
Cover Design and Book Layout by: - Angela Hardwick
Book Writing Structure: Randy E. Henderson

Mathews, Cory
Strength Through The Struggle
First Edition Print
ISBN 13: 978-1-939670-30-4
ISBN: 1-939670-30-4
Printed in the USA.

TABLE OF CONTENTS

CHAPTER 1

As far as I can remember, there was nothing easy about my childhood. I remember more difficult times than happy times. Although the difficult times seemed to be normal for me growing up. In 1975 my mother, Lisa Laney, was a fifteen-year-old high school student who used heavy drugs, such as marijuana, LSD, and pills. She would take the bus to and from school daily where she would soon meet a man named Walter Mathews, who was also the bus driver. Walter Mathews was a very sharp man, flashy and very smooth. He dressed with platform shoes, lots of jewelry and a perm hair style down to his shoulders. From that point on, they became a couple. He took her off the streets and got her off the drugs. Soon after, she found out she was pregnant with me. Nearly forced to have an abortion by both her mother and my father, she laid in the doctor's office but halfway through the procedure, she heard a voice say, "RUN!" She ran out of the doctor's office against my father and grandmother's will. Barefooted in a hospital gown, she ran and called a friend named Gail. She hid at Gail's house until it was too late to have an abortion. August 4th of 1976, I was born in Las Vegas, Nevada. My dad already had one son, who was just a couple years old. Three years later my mother found herself pregnant again with my sister. During this time, my mother and father would never marry.

As it seems, my first happy memory in life was going to Mount Charleston with my mother and father to play in the snow and inner tube down a hill. We had a fun time and all seemed well. Going to Head Start preschool, I can remember everyone at school getting ready for the Christmas season, with stockings, candy canes and a gentleman dressed up as Santa Clause. I also remember in the first grade, after lunch I would always have fifty cents to buy candy or popcorn. At the end of each day, the teachers would walk us to our buses and the buses would take us home. However, one day instead of following the teacher to get on the bus, I wondered off and got lost. Hours had past, the sun started to go down and it was getting dark. I was getting scared and felt lost, not knowing where I was until I saw my dad pull up. He gave me a big hug and we went home. It's a moment I'll never forget, because things at that point seemed to be as good as it was going to get.

My mother had cleaned herself up; she was completely sober. She was going to nursing school at a community college and later would work in the medical field. All the while, my dad was still driving the school bus but behind the scene, he was a hustler with the women and selling drugs. For as long as I could remember, even as a toddler, my dad would take me on his ten-speed bicycle throughout the neighborhood and sell drugs. To me that part of life was normal. In fact, I thought that's how all kids' families were. By the time, I was six years old I knew how to cook cocaine into rock form. I knew the difference between powder and freebase cocaine. I knew what nickel bags; dime bags and quarter bags were. I even knew what a kilo was. I'd see large quantities of money that only dad would count. He was an independent worker. I used to also watch him make counterfeit money. He knew how to make a one dollar bill look like a one-hundred-dollar bill. My dad had only a few guys in his circle. They did just about everything together. They had a van club. My dad's van was a very popular van around the city. It was green with gold flakes, a gold stripe on the side and the words "Macaroni Special" also painted along the side. His van was the coolest van to me. It had a TV, a refrigerator and some cool plush seats.

My dad and his friends would have all kinds of parties. Mostly I know they would smoke marijuana all the time and have lots of women. Usually my mom and I would be in the back room the whole night by ourselves, until my sister came along. At school I was very quiet but slowly came out of my shell. All my friends were older than me and in different grades, so I really had no one to talk to about all that was going on or to share secrets with. Usually my dad would let me ride on his bus with him picking up high school kids. So, between working on the bus, selling drugs and working women my dad was always viewed as a man who liked to make money. It would not be long, because eventually my dad would become addicted to his own devices, particularly the drugs that he sold. He would do anything to manipulate or get what he wanted. My mother would do all she could to protect and shield us from his lifestyle.

After a while the drug abuse would take its toll, and my dad became very abusive in the home toward my mother and me. I remember one day I stepped in and tried to stop my dad

2

from beating my mom, and that's when he turned and became very physically abusive to me. My dad was about six feet in height, close to two hundred pounds, and very muscular. In fact, this is where I get my muscular build. My dad became a different person. I began to see only what I thought to be the bad in him. And my mother lived her life in fear. One day she took my sister and me and we could move into an apartment, where he would eventually find us. She would escape again and we found ourselves moving from place to place to get away. Sometimes my mother would pick my sister and me up from school, and when we would get to our apartment my dad would be hiding in the closet. He would then jump out and chase us out of the house as we would scream for help. I started to keep my mom's kitchen knives in areas all throughout the apartment. I vowed that if he tried to get us again I would attempt to kill him with the knife. I used to stand on a chair looking through the peephole for hours wondering if my dad would show up. I was very afraid. By this time, I was in the third grade and we lived in a predominantly white side of town. Where I went to school, I was one of the few black kids. It was a whole different scenery for me than what I was used to. I became friends with the mayor's son and the sheriff's grandson, Zachery Moran. I also became friends with Benny Binion III. Binion's grandfather owned the casino Binion's Horseshoe in Las Vegas. Binion's grandfather would be murdered later. On the news, it was said that he had millions of dollars of silver and gold coins buried in the desert in Las Vegas.

Now I had lots of friends whose parents were rich and white. They never treated me any different. There was no racial tension. I would often spend weekends at their houses where we would ride skateboards and dirt bikes, or even go out to the desert and catch lizards. These became some of my favorite things to do. My mom had a friend name Melinda. Her husband Jerry offered to let us move in with them in their apartment in hopes to keep my dad from finding us and harassing us. My mom and Melinda worked at the Silver Slipper Casino where Melinda introduced my mom to a man named Wayne Brandon. He was a former minor league baseball player, and they eventually started dating. I wasn't very fond of him at first. I had a lot of anger built up inside of me from the way things went with my dad, so I hated any man being close to my mom. I use to write him letters and threaten to kill him if he didn't stop dating her. Later I realized how much of a blessing it was that he did not listen or regard these threatening letters I would write him every night. One day my dad came, knocking and banging on the Door, and I was so afraid. I dropped my knife and I cried. Wayne came and hugged me, then went outside and he and my dad exchanged words. My dad was very bad on drugs and he didn't even look the same. Wayne began to push and shove him around and my dad ran off. This would be the last I would see of my father for a very long time. At that very moment I was relieved of every bit of fear I had and I was comforted by Wayne's security. From then on, I accepted him in our lives.

Wayne had come from a very large family and was the fifth of eleven brothers and sisters. They were very classy people. My mom and Wayne were married in 1987, one year after they had started dating. I soon started calling him dad. At this point my grades weren't too good, so Wayne would often have to help and teach me. I must give a lot of credit to him, even now. He taught me a lot about being a man. He taught me how to have class and how to have edict. However, my anger had nowhere else to go but out, and trouble soon arose.

CHAPTER 2

When I was eleven years old, things were looking up for my family. My mom had found a good job working for a good dentist. However, although things were working out for my mom, my life began to take a whole different twist. My anger that had built up over the years was letting loose. I would often find myself in lots of trouble with my mom and new stepdad, whom I did admire. My anger would become more obvious by the day. In addition to my anger, I would hear a voice in my head that would confront me about the way I felt. My mom was raised as a Buddhist and my stepfather had no understanding of a relationship with God. He did not believe in church. So, when I went to them and explained to them about the voice I would hear, they were overwhelmingly concerned and sought medical advice. So, I went to see a physiatrist and was diagnosed bipolar, manic depressive and schizophrenic. I was prescribed to take medications such as Prozac, Depakote and Paxil. When I look back in hindsight, it was only the voice of God that I would become familiar with years later. The medicines that I was taking never appeased my anger, but it seemed that they did put an end to the voice. However, there were times of calm in my life. Since before I could remember I was always picking up lizards and frogs, and looking at reptile books at the library, so my mother would often buy me reptiles from the local pet store. I was no ordinary kid. I never cared too much for the playground but I loved lizards and reptiles. This fascination with reptiles often took my mind to positive places.

Since my stepfather was big into sports, he was the first to encourage me to play. Sports became a temporary solution for my anger issues. It was a way that I would be able to socialize with other kids. My favorite sport was football. I also played baseball and would later even run track. It was very evident that I was stronger than my other peers. I loved to be physical; I played corner back, safety and running back on the football teams. Then when I was twelve years old we moved again, closer to my old neighborhood where I rekindled with my old friends. We'd run the streets and I had started being a very wild child, hanging with my old friends. My mother and I got into various arguments. One time it got so bad that I ran away from home. I made my way to downtown Las Vegas on Fremont Street. Fremont Street was a hustler's paradise. It was where you could find prostitutes, drugs, murders and pickpocketing of lots of tourist. So, to survive, I started selling drugs through a friend of mine, Anthony Glenn, who was a big shot in the neighborhood. He was a big-time hustler who had lots of money, drugs and guns, and lots of people looked up to him. Anthony was 27 years old and became like a big brother or even a father figure to most of us youngsters in the street. He showed me the ropes. He made sure that I knew how to be sharp in the streets and made me go back to school.

Back then if you wanted to be big time, usually you got drugs from Cuban drug lords or Mexican cartels. Anthony would deal with them, but he was more of the independent type. At one point I was put into juvenile hall, and was charged as a runaway. I also had a battery and assault with a deadly weapon charge. My mom came to see me, and the judge released me back to her custody. However, I found myself going back to Fremont and spending more time trying to make money. Eventually, there were two prostitutes whose names were Vivian and Star. They took care of me and treated me like I was their own child, but they also treated me like I was the boss. They hustled for me and sold my drugs. I remember one night I was staying in a motel room, and Vivian came to me and said there was a guy outside who wanted to buy one hundred dollars' worth of drugs. So, I gave her the drugs and told her to take care of the guy. He paid her with a one-hundred-dollar bill but when she gave the money to me, I immediately knew the money was counterfeit. In my mind, I knew that there was only one person who made counterfeit money that way. Vivian did not know who the guy was and I went to go after him, but he was already in a cab and gone. I had people search for him and days later she found him at the Ambassador Hotel. He wanted to buy more drugs. Vivian came and told me she found the man I was looking for, so I took the liberty of making the deal myself. When I walked into the room, I looked at the man in his eyes and said, "Dad, it's me, Cory." At that moment, I did not know if I wanted to kill him or run away. I was seeing someone whom I had hated for years. At first, he didn't recognize me. Once he did, he was so shameful of me seeing him that way, but because I was all about the money, I sold him drugs. He became one of my best customers, until I got in trouble once again.

Back in the neighborhood, my friends and I were hanging out drinking and smoking weed. We saw a couple of rich kids at a convenient store and we robbed them of their clothes, wallets, Walkman's or any other merchandise they had. I was arrested and sentenced to six months in Spring Mountain Youth Camp for Boys. Though it was supposed to be hard time, I had lots of fun there. I saw lots of my friends from my neighborhood and had lots of respect from other gang members. I thought to do something constructive to make my time go by faster, so I began to run track and started weight lifting. I became hooked on the weights and spent more time in the weight room than any of my peers. On the day, I was released, it just so happened to be the beginning of the Rodney King riots which would turn into a gang peace treaty. It was the weirdest thing I'd ever seen. Bloods and Crips hanging together, and putting all their hatred and animosity aside. But this treaty did not last long, especially being that the guys from my neighborhood were never comfortable being around Bloods. We were the Crips. And I guess you can say we were absolute trouble makers. So, when the opportunity arose to separate ourselves from other gangs, we made it very clear that we hated everybody.

Now my mother was working for a dentist, and I needed my wisdom teeth pulled. After they were pulled I was taken to my mom's house to rest. My friends came over to comfort me with some weed and alcohol. All my friends loved my mother; it was as if she was their mother. She was often giving advice and she would pretty much do just about everything she could to keep me within her sight, even if it meant allowing my friends and I to stay and spend many nights in her home. It was kind of funny. There would be a house full of killers and fugitives. When my stepdad would come home from work, he'd have to step over machine guns and all kinds of weapons. We'd sleep a lot during the day; we'd be passed out on the couch and the floor. At night, we'd do gangster business. Eventually my step dad became fed up with my mom because she put up with us, but at the same time he was frightened to say anything to us, and just let it go.

When my friends and I would go out, we'd do pretty much anything and almost everything to get money; extortion, robbery, and selling drugs just to name a few. We were a band of brothers. We were guilty of bank robberies and were responsible for most of the gun play that you would hear about in North Las Vegas. Most times we'd go across town, and rob Foot Lockers and convenient stores. However, the night I had my teeth pulled out we robbed three convenient stores, one of them being a 7-Eleven. I was heavily medicated and high on pain meds because of my tooth extraction. I was feeling woozy by the time we robbed the third store and I did not want to go in, so I decided to stay in the car while my friends went into the 7-Eleven and attempted to rob it. About a minute or so later, my friends came running out of the store with no money. I knew what needed to be done. I cussed them all out, took our gun and ran back into the store. The cashier wouldn't open the register; she thought we were a bunch of kids with a toy gun. Although we were bunch of kids, the gun was very real. She had already been on the phone with the police, so I shot the gun in the air and pointed it at her. It was then that she finally opened the register and gave me the money. I proceeded to run out of the store. The car we were driving was a '78 Chevy Nova. My friends had taken me to my mom's house, but because no one was there I was locked out. So, we drove over the hill to another house that we hung out at in my neighborhood but the police were waiting on us. Because of our ages, we were all taken to juvenile hall and were charged with robbery with the use of a deadly weapon. I was still on probation since being released from the youth prison, so it wasn't looking good for me.

It just so happened that the dentist my mother had worked for, who had also performed my surgery, was at a political dinner party with big time lawyers and judges. When he found out that I was incarcerated, he asked one of the lawyers if he could help me out. They called my stepfather and asked if my mom was ok. The word had gotten around to a big-time mob lawyer named David Chessnoff, who was also partners with Oscar Goodman. David Chessnoff had friends who played softball with my stepfather, so he was very familiar with my family and who I was. He agreed to help me and took my case pro bono. David came into the juvenile hall to visit me. He demanded all the clothes I wore that night and told me to keep quiet. When we went to court, none of the witnesses had the same story, so David Chessnoff ate them for lunch. I walked out with no cuffs and no convictions. David called me into his office and there sat my New York Yankees jacket. That was the only thing that linked me to the crime. He said as a payment, I could let him have that jacket and as far as I know, he kept it for years later. He was a good friend to the family.

I continued to commit other crimes. I would rob big time drug dealers, one who at the time was Don Houston. We put him in the trunk of his own car and took him out to the desert where we threatened to kill him if he didn't tell us where the drugs and money were. He wouldn't break for a while and this almost led to a night of torture for him. Finally, he gave in and we left him in the middle of the desert in the cold of the night, duct taped and without any clothes. On other occasions, we'd car jack people, mostly at red lights. We would hit the back of someone's car and when they got out to see what the problem was, we'd point our guns at them. We'd make them get on the ground, search them and then take their car. We'd then take the car to our neighborhood and have it striped down. It would take us less than three minutes to strip the car. Then we'd sell whatever we got out of it, whether it'd be rims, music stereo systems, or hydro licks. Back in those days, if you drove a nice low rider you were pretty much a target, just like if you drove around and wore blue, you were automatically assumed to be affiliated with Crips and could get killed on the spot. If you wore a lot of jewelry or even a pager you were assumed to be a drug dealer. Most people would say it was the police who were prejudiced, but we were prejudiced against our own kind.

In those days, being in the early '90s, gang war was at an all-time high in the streets of Las Vegas. We did lots of drive-by's to make a name for ourselves. There were a handful of us who grew up in the neighborhood known as the Regal Estates in North Las Vegas. This was our turf. This was where we controlled everything. You had to be one of us if you wanted to sell drugs there or even talk to the girls in our neighborhood. And though we were surrounded by other neighborhoods with rival gangs, we felt safe on our own turf. Life was all about respect, fear, drugs, money, and women. Just as much as we were selling drugs, we would have our own drug habits as well. We smoked lots of weed, angel dust, and sherm. By the time most of us turned fourteen we had already become somewhat alcoholics and drug addicts. We knew how to operate and use heavy artillery and weapons such as machine guns and assault rifles with great skill. Sherm seemed to be the preferred drug of choice for all of us in the neighborhood. This was a cigarette that was dipped in embalming fluid and wrapped in aluminum foil. When we smoked it some of us would feel hot, and people would take their clothes off in the middle of the street and run as if they were running for their lives. At other times the same drug made us feel like we had super powers. This is when we'd look to start fights with anybody, including the police. This would always end with ten officers stomping you, spraying you with mace, Tasing you and hitting you with billy clubs. One night all of us went to Circus Circus. This was a family casino, a place for kids to play arcade games and watch a circus show. Of course, we were high and smoked sherm before we arrived. As soon as we got there I saw a member from the Blood gang and there was an immediate brawl. The police came in, broke up the fight, and threatened to 86 us off the property and take us to jail. I was so high on sherm that I thought I was a super robot and refused to surrender to them. It took just about every police officer in that casino to take me down. I was sent to juvenile and released that night. Each time I was in juvenile hall I'd get letters from the big homies who were in prison. They would often tell me how much respect they had for me and how proud of me they were. I felt accepted. All the guys I looked up to were in prison, and now some of the guys had begun looking up to me.

CHAPTER 3

I was part of a gang called the North Town Gangster Crips. There weren't that many of us but we were rumored to be over thousands deep, with lots of killers. We had a notorious reputation of being violent and I had begun to do everything that I could to uphold that reputation. I was known in the streets as Madness. I fed into the reputation by striking fear throughout the streets. The cops had it out for us bad, but mostly just for me. I was also known to be a jack artist, so most drug dealers would do their best to avoid me. Eventually people began to tattletale on our activities. There was a well-known drug dealer who was a member of the Bloods (our rival gang). His name was Keith Carter. Little did we know that he was an informant for the Feds. One day I set out to rob him, and I took his drugs and money only to find out later that his house was bugged and the police were listening the entire time. Though they didn't catch me there, they surrounded my mother's house later. I escaped and hid at my homeboy's house.

Now, I was on the run and wanted by the police. I couldn't go home and I was unsafe in my own neighborhood because the police were swarming through the streets day in and day out looking for me. Eventually, my money had begun to run low as I was going from motel to motel on the Las Vegas strip. Two of my best friends, T Bone and Smoke, had stood by my side and we did what we had to do to survive. Both of my friends had already been to jail for murder and people feared us. We called ourselves 3 The Hard Way. An opportunity came for us to meet a friend of ours in Los Angeles who would give us new drivers' licenses, social security cards, and birth certificates. We needed new identities bad. We were all wanted. However, on the way to California we were on the freeway and saw one of the Blood members driving alongside of us. I hated this particular Blood member with a passion. His name was 10 Ounce. I began to point my gun out of the window, along with my friends, and we began to shoot, intending to kill him. He crashed his car, the whole while an animal control officer driving behind us. He was reporting the whole thing to the police. We drive as far as we could and try to exit the freeway, but there was a police barricade. We drive the car through the barricade and the car stalls. So, we all jumped out of the car and ran on foot, followed by the police helicopter that filmed the entire event. My friend, Smoke, ran into a family's home and held them hostage. Now, I was only sixteen years old but because of the rumors that had been spreading in the street, everyone thought that I was a huge monster, terrorizing the streets. We were caught by the police and when I told the officer my name, he didn't believe me; the fact that I was Cory Mathews. Before I was put away into the police car I sat on the ground with my hair braided in corn rows. I felt that the only way that I could get out of this mess was either my enemies would kill me in prison or I would die some glorious gang death.

I was a very depressed young man with suicidal thoughts and I didn't want to live anymore. When I was taken to the detention center where my prints and picture were taken, the police finally realized who I was. Because of my age, I was moved to the juvenile hall facility and put in a room with detectives that wanted me to give up my friends. I refused and made up all kinds of stories and lies to get them off my back, at least for the night. Being emotionally and physically drained from hours of their investigations, I remember crying in my cell asking the Lord to take the pain away that I had inside for so long. Early on as a child I had a history of talking to the Lord. This was the first time I had talked to him since I was put on medication in 1987. I knew the things I had done were wrong and I was willing to accept my punishment.

From then on, my time in the juvenile detention center seemed only to be like a vacation. Special privileges were given to me. I was able to lift weights and watch lots of TV. I was feared among the other kids and that began to feed my ego. I wanted people to know I was just as bad as I seemed to be. The administrators at the detention center and the gang members weren't getting along and two administrators by the names of Mr. McCloud and Mr. Campbell had taken a liking to me. They felt like I could bring peace and calm to the gangs in the facility. If I was ever upset they'd go out of their way to let me have a radio in my room so I could listen to whatever music I wanted. Once a week a former Harlem Crip gang member named Greg Atkins would come in and do gang interventions with forty to fifty of us children who were gang members. He had been to prison, yet he had turned his life around and made every effort to help the children. Because of his influence on myself and the other kids, Mr. McCloud set up a private meeting between Greg and me. Though he wasn't a spiritual person, he said the only way he would help me out was if I turned my life around just like he did.

In 1994 I went before the judge and he said that because of the extent of my crimes I had to be charged and certified as an adult. Now I would be moving to the Clark County Detention Center. I had four counts of kidnapping, numerous accounts of use with a deadly weapon, robbery, home invasions, bodily harm, and the list goes on. I was expecting to go to prison for the rest of my life and just accept it as punishment from God. I was placed in a closed custody module where all the murders, robbers and gang members spend their time in jail. There was no protection or restraints, and I was the youngest guy in the module, yet I walked around like I owned the place. Other older Crips who had respected me took care of me and made sure that I was ok. They gave me a nickname while I was in jail; they called me the Pepsi Generation, which was their way of saying that I was a beginning of a new generation of gangsters. I was constantly getting into fights and being put into the hole.

One day Greg Atkins came to visit me. He would always send messages to my girlfriends on the streets and do everything he could to help me out. He said to me, "You've got to stop getting into trouble. Every time you get into trouble the judge will see it in the courtroom, and you don't want the judge to see anything bad." What he said was like a light bulb moment for me. On one hand, I knew I'd be in prison for the rest of my life, but the more Greg talked with me, there had begun to be a slight hope that maybe there was a chance that I could get out. Until that time, however, the very same detectives that interrogated me when I was in juvenile hall found out that I had lied to them and I didn't give them the information that they wanted. They were furious with me. One of them told me that they were going to make it so bad for me that I would die in prison, and that their great grandchildren would be born before I'd ever get a chance to see daylight. I couldn't hold my cool any longer, so I just lost it. I didn't have a single kind world to say to them as I cussed at them and spit at them behind the glass, making sure that everyone in the facility knew how much I hated them.

Now with all this going on, there were things going on outside the jail on the streets. The police who had my case were also set up as gang units, and they began to have a TV show where they filmed everything they did. This show was called The Nasty Boys. Only those of us who ran the streets and did dirt knew that The Nasty Boys were just a crooked police department. They would do drug busts and gang raids. I remember there was a Crip in North Las Vegas who went by the name of Ezack who was shot in the head and killed. Though it looked like gang rivalry, everyone in the street suspected The Nasty Boys were the ones who killed Ezack, yet no one could prove the allegations. This cause the gangs in the street to build up an animosity toward the police. A few of these officers, one of whom we called Robo Cop, another Johnny Armstrong, and Officer Calvin Butts just to name a few, went out of their way to threaten my family daily. On a regular basis, they would kick in my mother and stepfather's door and put guns to their, heads as well as my baby sister. They'd hold them hostage and make statements that if I ever saw the streets again, they would make sure an accident would happen to me. They also said they had connections on the inside and that I wouldn't survive a day in prison. I had no clue about this at the time, but with my mother's fear for my life she visited me and explained all this to me. I asked Greg to protect them, and he went even further than that and got us a lawyer. Still though, my hostility escalated and I sent word out to all my friends on the street to keep an eye out on them.

By this point, there was an unexpected twist in my case. An arrangement was set where I went to court, they explained my rights and set a hearing date. At the preliminary hearing word, had gotten to me that there would be no witnesses, for they were too frightened to testify against me. Everything I had done to put fear in the hearts of people was now coming into play. There was a great code in the street that we lived by, and that was NO SNITCHING! If you snitched or told on someone, your street credit would go down the drain, you would eventually see the person you snitched on in jail and the tables would be turned on you. After my preliminary hearing, not only did they not have enough evidence to keep me but none of the victims showed up to court as expected. The state requested a thirty-day continuance to give them an opportunity to contact and gather up the witnesses and victims, and go further with the proceedings. Even still, the thirty days came and went, and no witnesses or victims were found. So thus, the judge ordered me to be released on my own recognizance. I immediately went to my old neighborhood before even talking to my mom or my family, and there we had a meeting to let everyone know that there was going to be war on the streets.

CHAPTER 4

I was only out of jail for five days now, hanging out with a couple of my friends, Sporty Corty and Blue Devil. Since I was fresh out of jail, Blue Devil had an idea to buy some pizza; we would all eat pizza and get drunk and high. However, when we got to Pizza Hut, Blue Devil went in only to rob the place. He came out and offered Sporty Corty and me wallets and such, and of course a pizza. We then headed back to our neighborhood, though right as we pulled onto the street the cops came behind us. As we came to a complete stop we all got out of the car to run. Eventually Sporty Corty and I got caught. Now Sporty Corty wasn't anything like us. He was just a preppy guy who was on the honor roll and got good grades. His parents bought him his first car. He wasn't a gangster, like we were. So, when the police had him in handcuffs he began trying his hardest to explain to the police that he didn't have anything to do with the robbery. The truth was neither one of us knew that Blue Devil was going in to rob the place. The police didn't believe anything, which wasn't surprising because I was a known criminal and had the likely personality and arrest record with other similar charges. So, we went to jail. I was charged with twelve counts of robbery, but I wasn't even identified as the robber who held everyone at gun point. Two weeks later the police arrested Blue Devil, he was identified, and I was released from jail once again.

During this two-week period of my incarceration, my shady doings on the street were finding their way back to my family. The guy that I had robbed in the past, Keith Carter, had found my little sister, held her at gun point and threatened to kill her if she didn't send me a message that there was going to be bloodshed when I got out of jail. That was his way of saying he wanted to kill me. I got furious. A girlfriend of mine hooked me up with her ex-boyfriend who could get me any weapon I wanted. So, I purchased a MAC-11, TEC-9 with a silencer, a 380 and a Glock 9. A silent war was on as I drove through the street looking for anyone I was offended by. Rumors even spread to the police that I was aiming to kill a certain group of officers who would kick in my mother's door and hold my family at gun point. Now the police were very hot on the street looking for me again. So, I just laid low, though every night the police would come through my neighborhood, put some of my homeboys in

16

handcuffs and threaten to arrest them if they didn't give information on my whereabouts. I praise God now that nothing I had planned had turned out, whether it was against the police, Keith Carter or other enemies during that time. The fact was that Keith Carter was still an informant for the police and though he threatened my sister, I was never able to demonstrate my anger against him, for he had went to church, got baptized and started walking the straight and narrow.

Time went on and a buddy of mine, Big Dave, had made a lot of money smuggling and selling drugs in prison. His brother, Piggy, helped. He was a big time high roller. He sold lots of drugs to many of the gang members. Piggy was feared and very dangerous. One day, his own enemies shot him and he ended up paralyzed in a wheel chair. Piggy was always Dave's way of getting drugs into prison. As our collaborations grew, my loyalty to my big homeboys in prison would become a very big deal. Since I was on the street making a name for myself, my homeboys asked if I could help them bring drugs into prison, just like Piggy and Dave. So, whenever the visiting days would come, I would have my mom sneak little balloons of cocaine and marijuana into the visiting room to give to my homeboys. For Piggy and my mom both, it was always easy for them to smuggle drugs into prison. They wouldn't even search Piggy because he was in a wheel chair, and because my mother was a woman, she could hide the drugs in various places within the privacy of her own body. Another common way was to swallow the drugs while they were wrapped up tight in a balloon or plastic, and once inside of the prison, you'd stick your finger down your throat and vomit it up. This operation ran very smoothly. My big homeboys in prison were well taken care of and I was given respect and authority as I continued to make a name for myself on the streets. Piggy had taken a very strong liking to me. He needed me with my reputation to help him solidify his empire. I'd watch his back day in and day out, and go everywhere with him to make sure he was ok. Because I'd help him smuggle the drugs into prison and move drugs on the street, I had a limited supply for myself.

Piggy came to me one day saying he overheard a lot of people speaking about the fact that they wanted their revenge on me, and that many people wanted to kill me. I was a marked man. So, I told him about my arsenal of weapons and that if something were to ever go down, I always stayed ready. He called me a couple of days later and told me to come to his house; he had a gift for me. I'd always admired Piggy because of the money he had and the respect he was given on the street, so I was eager to see what he had for me. When I got to Piggy's house he gave me a box, and inside of it there was a sawed-off AK-47 assault rifle with a fold out knife that extended from the barrel. Not to motion there was a fifth-round clip, a ninety-round clip and boxes of ammunition. This was a token of appreciation because Piggy was going back to California and would not see me for a long time. Although, he wouldn't tell me why he was going back to California. All he said was, "Try not to tear down any telephone poles with my new chopper." The gift made me very excited.

One of my first times using the gun, I was driving through the neighborhood and one of the Blood members was throwing up their gang signs. I got out of the car and began shooting at random. Luckily, no one got killed that day. Another time was when we were in the heart of the Blood territory at a night club called Chey's Place. On Saturday nights, this became a hub for many gang members throughout the city. Everyone knew that all the fine girls would be there. My friend, Terrance, and I were out in the parking lot where I was leaning up against my car when suddenly hundreds of Bloods began to swarm us. The guy leading the pack was named Andre Stampton and just so happened to be Terrance's cousin. Terrance supposed that maybe he could talk to his cousin to keep things from getting out of hand because we were clearly out numbered. But before any peace could be brought about, one of the Blood members hit Terrance in the head. Terrance was knocked out, laying in his own puddle of blood, and as I reached to get my gun from the car, I also was knocked out from behind.

CHAPTER 5

I was awakened due to the various stomps and kicks from countless Blood members. I prepared myself to die. One of the Blood members whom they called Snow had taken my 9-millimeter gun that I was reaching for prior to being knocked out. He had cocked the gun and pressed it against my forehead, right between my eyes. He began to pull the trigger multiple times. I heard the gun go, "click, click, click," but there were no shots fired. Snow got angry because the gun seemed to be jammed up and not working. He slammed the gun down onto the ground and began cussing, as the rest of them continued to beat me and stomp me in the head, and all over the rest of my body. I began to think within myself, if I could get up and get a distance from them I could be ok. At that very moment we all looked up to see flashing police lights coming at us with their sirens on. All the Bloods took off running. Terrance was laying down, still knocked out cold. I suppose the police went after the Bloods. They did not help us. However, a couple of girls from across the parking lot ran over to help. I looked all around for the police, but there weren't any around. The girls said they didn't see any police even come. I felt that maybe the police were angels. I thought about how the gun did not go off, and how there was plenty of opportunity for the Bloods to kill me. I didn't know if Terrance was dead or alive, but then I found him still breathing with a heartbeat. I asked the two girls if they could take him to the hospital. They replied, "What about you?" I said, "No, I'll be fine." I could drive home full of rage and vengeance on my mind, only imagining what I was going to do to those Bloods. They should've killed me when they had the chance. Now things were going to get bad.

Covered in blood with my eye busted wide open, I walked into my mother's house. As soon as I opened the door, my mother stood at the top of the stairs with a look of distress and worry on her face. She knew something was wrong. It was as if God had kept her up all night with the feeling that something bad had happened to her son. I brushed her off and pushed past her into my bedroom where I had lots of guns and arsenal underneath the mattress of my bed. I picked up two clips and put the AK-47 in a pillow case, along with two hand guns in my waist. Heading down the stairs I saw my mother crying and begging me not to leave the house. I almost didn't go.

Seeing her like that did not sit easy with me. Something was in the back of my mind telling me I had to change and I should get out now, while I was still alive. But because I thrived on people fearing me, I didn't want my enemies to think they could get away with what they had done to me. At the same time, three cars pulled up to the front of my mother's house as I was leaving. My big home boy, Ty Bud, led the caravan. Ty Bud was a cold-blooded killer and one of the original founders of the North Town Gangster Crips, who I was a part of. He was a lot older than us, and everyone in the street feared and respected him. He asked me if I was ok. Word had gotten around that Terrance and I had been jumped and left for dead. I told him Terrance was on his way to the hospital and I didn't know his condition. I told him that I was on my way to kill those guys that jumped Terrance and me. They saw my pillow case and immediately they knew what time it was. I jumped into Ty Bud's car and we drove back to Chey's Place looking for the Bloods. Not one of them was found, so we got out and walked the streets to make our presence known. Some of the Blood girls in the parking lot began to mouth off to us. People ducked to the ground as I pulled out my AK-47 and began shooting, sending them a very strong message; that there was war.

We went back to our neighborhood to hide out. I was still covered in blood and had lots of pain in my eye. I refused to go to the doctor though. Instead, I put a towel over my eye as we all smoked Sherm. The higher I got, the less pain I felt. Morning came and went. As the afternoon came around, my mother still had not slept. She found out where I was and came to the house crying and begging for me to come home. Because I was so angry and hostile I told her I couldn't come home, at least not yet. As she left though, the look on her face struck me in my conscience. I wondered if that would be the very last time I would ever see my mother. It bothered me deeply. I knew I was very wrong.

Eventually, we got word that our friend, Terrance, was doing ok. He only had a gash on the side of his head, and he was stitched up and ready to go. As night fell upon us, we got high some more and went out looking for the Bloods again. Their neighborhood was like a ghost town. We couldn't find one single Blood, so to let them know we had been there, we shot up homes, apartments, cars and all kinds of buildings. Night after night it was as if they were hiding from us. One night while we were roaming through the Bloods neighborhood looking for them, the police got behind us. We turned the corner in attempt to ditch them and my friend, Spoony Loc, took the guns, jumped out of the car and ran to hide in the desert. We finally pulled over for the police and they gave us a hard time. They asked all kinds of questions, like what were we doing in that area, but eventually they let us go. They said we didn't belong in that neighborhood and we responded with a lie, saying "We were going to find our girlfriends."

Weeks passed and my friends went to hang out at the Moulin Rouge Nightclub, which was a popular spot for drug dealers on the West Side. This night, I was not with my friends but stayed at home. I remember as I sat down to watch TV in the wee hours of night, I saw on the news that the Moulin Rouge Nightclub had been shot up. There were multiple homicides. Surely this was a result of a continuing war between those Bloods and us Crips. While I was watching the news, I had a happy gut feeling that my homeboys had lit up the whole place. While some of them were arrested, I laid low for a bit longer because the police continued to swarm though the neighborhoods looking for any suspicious gang activity. From time to time Bloods would come to our neighborhood trying to talk to the girls but we would shoot out the street lights with our guns so that we could have the advantage in case anyone coming in or out of our neighborhood did not belong there. So, at night it would be pitch black and we would often be hiding in drug houses or sometimes even behind cars in driveways. We'd often shoot at Bloods as they tried to cruise through. More and more people were dying in the streets and gang life was only getting worse. One night, we caravanned to a movie theater a few cars loads deep. The car in front of the car I was driving belonged to another gang called the White Street Mafia. They pulled up next to my homeboys that were in front of us and began to shoot through the window, then they speed off. My homeboy, Isacc, had gotten killed that night. Watching my homeboy get killed was extremely upsetting. He was now the third of my homeboys to get killed, after Lil Mike and Gerald. The gang war only increased. We were at war with numerous gangs. My homeboys and I had to live with the fact that there would be no rest or peace until our enemies were gone.

I was very depressed. I started snorting a lot of cocaine and ended up being in places where lots of women were drawn to me. I had my dad's gift of being a smooth talker and the ladies loved my long silky hair. I carried myself as if I owned the streets, so wherever I went I was into something. Around this time in my life I met a lady named Alicia, who had many connections with high rollers. She was a 29-year-old diva and I was an 18-year-old thug. I remember telling my friend, Clinky, to pull over so I could talk to her. She was coming out of a local store, and I knew that she would be mine. I mentioned to her that a woman like herself belonged to a man like me, but she of course, at the same time was thinking she had more to offer me than I had for her. We exchanged numbers and soon became close until she became my girlfriend. I still saw my friends in the street, but my street binges became less and less. Being with Alicia was a new experience for me. The first time I waked into her home I noticed a coffee table stacked with Rob Report magazines. These were magazines of merchandise for the wealthy. Every day she and I would read one. It was her way of teaching me undercover. Now I was learning about diamonds, suits, and luxury cars.

Though I was young and immature, I was changing. Alicia wanted to go on a cruise and take a vacation trip to the Bahamas, so we started making plans. A week before we were set to leave on the vacation, I went on a drug run to purchase some drugs because I still had a habit. I ended up running into some of my old enemies from the Gerson Park. We got into a shootout and I ran out of bullets. I jumped into my truck and sped out of there as if my life depended on it. This sure wasn't my night, as I was being chased by the Gersons a few more blocks down, out of ammunition, my truck runs out of gas. I had to then jump out of the truck and run for my life.

I could get away from the Gersons by jumping over fences and peoples' backyards. I made it a couple more blocks and saw my homeboy's car parked in front of the gas station. So, I ran in there and told my homeboy the situation I was in. I explained to him that I needed to get back to my truck with some gas. He had the nerve to refuse to help me. He thought that I was high and the drugs had taken their toll. He offended me by saying, "You just don't know when to quit do you? You need to lay off the drugs!" This angered me like no other, because if it wasn't for me he wouldn't have even had the success he had in being one of the biggest drug dealers around. It was me who gave him a dope package when he got out of prison and told him to get on his feet. It was me who had his back which meant no one would mess with him because he was my partner. So, without any help, I had to leave my truck until the next day.

That following night, a couple of my homeboys and I were getting high all the way until the morning approached. All the while I was very upset, even to the point of me burning inside, in that my homeboy, Clinky, refused to help me and treated me like I was some bum off the street. So, I drive up to one of his drug houses. I knew his routine; where he would be, when he would be gone and when he'd come back. I then broke into the house and stole twenty thousand cash and a quarter kilo of cocaine. Just moments later my pager was going off. It was Clinky paging me 911, 911. Immediately I thought he knew that I had robbed him but I didn't want to make myself look suspicious, so I pulled to a pay phone as calm as I could be and called him. He was very upset and went on explaining to me how he had been robbed of his money and his drugs, and now he needed my help. Now the tables had turned. He thought that it was a group of guys that were going around robbing dope dealers and he wanted to put their heads to rest. I told him that I was unable to help him now and distanced myself from him. He never knew that it was me all along.

At the end of this week, Alicia and I had taken our vacation to the Bahamas. For four days and three nights I could relax and have peace while sailing over the ocean in a cruise ship. It was the first time that I had ever been on a cruise, let alone that far away from my own neighborhood. During it all, we saw the comedian, Sinbad, and we went on several excursions. I remember being able to see thirty feet down under the waters, and looked at all the fish and marine life. It brought me back to a suppressed memory in my childhood when I was into animals. I would catch bugs on the sidewalk and lizards in the desert. I kept saying how I wanted to jump in the water and catch some jellyfish and starfish with my own hands.

In the islands of the Bahamas where we would port, there was a girl on every corner who solicited to braid my hair. It was like that was there hustle. Of course, I was able to run into some thugs. One guy had a trash bag full of marijuana. So, while the lady was braiding my hair, I was talking to the guy about selling me some weed. Then I was able to get high in the Bahamas.

CHAPTER 6

By the time, we got back to the states, it was back to business as usual and I was back on the grind. I didn't want to continue robbing or selling drugs to make a living. I began searching for new opportunities to stack my money. Alicia would always make me feel comfortable and safe. I didn't have to worry as much when I was with her, surely a way to keep me around. She would get nice jewelry for me. For my nineteenth birthday, I was surprised with some diamond earrings. Being around her, I was being introduced to some of the finer things in life. I was slowly being introduced to some of her friends, some of whom had lots of money. I also encountered new friends of my own, mostly pimps. When you hear the word "pimp," you automatically assume this is some guy that beats women and forces them to do drugs and sell their bodies. But this was by far a misdiagnosed stereotype. These guys did not want their women doing drugs. In fact, they didn't even beat their women. They treated pimping and hoeing as if it was a business. And to come with all the big business was luxury, and the finest things in life. All these guys cared about was money and big possessions.

One of the guys named J Money drove around in a Rolls Royce, Excalibur and a Jaguar. He was a very classy man. I kept my eye on him, only to eventually begin to mimic his ways. He would go to the gym during the daytime to play basketball. At night, he would go to the salon to get his perm fixed up with a manicure and pedicure. He had two women who lived in a villa at the Caesar's Palace. He was spoiled with lots of money. He owned big real estates, both in Miami and Hawaii. Though I began to change, this classy new crowd was often still unsure about me, afraid that my gangster lifestyle had not died off yet. In all actuality, they were very right. My ties to the neighborhood were still strong and I held strong political power in the streets. My words held weight and whatever I said or requested would stand. My reputation over the years was nothing short of a notorious angry Crip. Lots of my friends at that time would be in and out of prison, so it almost became natural for me to spend more time in the neighborhood and in the street and less time with Alicia. She hated it, but understood at the same time.

My cousin and one of my best friends, George, was released out of prison from a five-year sentence for a robbery around this time. We were more like brothers. So, when he got out of prison, I took it upon myself to make sure that he was set and that he wouldn't have to work for anything. I gave him a dope package, some money and a new gun. I introduced George to my new lifestyle, in hopes that he would want to do big things and be all about money, where we would no longer have to hang out on the corner in the neighborhood, or rob people. All we had to do now was give the drugs to the youngsters and let them do the work for us, and without a doubt, we would always have women to make sure we were paid in full. We had the mentality already to be extreme in everything we did.

One week after George was let out of prison, another homeboy of mine named K Dogg had just been released as well, so we partied like it was nobody's business, drinking Cognac and snorting cocaine. My drug addictions weren't noticeable; however, it was a problem. George picked up on my drug habit and said he wanted to try the cocaine. The thing about cocaine was that it makes you feel like the coolest person in the world. It amplified your personality. It was a very social drug. The thing about George was he couldn't handle the drugs or liquor too well. One night, he turned into a totally different person. He still had a prison mentality and had yet to adjust to the way the streets have changed since he had been locked up. He went into prison at a young age and came out when he was 23 years old. Nothing was the same. A new wave of gangsters was out and everyone was trying to outrank one another. I was what you call a cross breed gangster. I was one of the old ones and had been around for a while, but I had stripes and the new generation of youngsters feared and respected me. Things were much worse at that time than before George had went to prison. Now that he was drunk and high, he became violent and began to threaten people all night. Little did I know that things would take a turn for the worse for him that night.

My friend, Ty Budd, George and myself went to the Heritage Lounge to get a snort of cocaine. After all the clubs, would shut down, everyone would migrate there and it became a spot where drug dealers, pimps and prostitutes would hang out. It was a big night and a drug dealer named Pinky had fat sacks of cocaine he was letting people try to promote his business. So, as we had all gotten high, George had begun to make violent threats against Pinky and they exchanged words with each other. George pulled out his pistol and threatened to pistol-whip Pinky in the head. Everyone in the place knew that George was just high, he needed to calm down and he would be fine in the morning. But Pinky took great offense. He snuck off to the pay phone, made a phone call and left. A short while later we were all outside in the parking lot. I went over to my car to talk to a young lady while Ty Budd and George stood on the sidewalk in front of the Heritage Lounge. A car pulled up close to George and Ty Budd, and whoever was in the car rolled down their windows and began to shoot. I thought to myself, "Aww, cuz!" I ran over there and George had his gun in his hand as if he were getting ready to shoot, only he was lying on the ground gasping for air. Everything happened so fast.

George had died in my arms, and the gunman sped off long before I could get there. Ty Budd took the gun from George's hand to hide it because we knew the police were coming. I began to scream and cry, feeling guilty. When the authorities came, they covered George in a white sheet. My uncle, Big George, came to identify his son. I looked him in the eye and hugged him as tight as I could as he began to scream, "My son! My son!" It was very hard on all of us. Images from that night stayed with me and haunted me for years, seeing George gasping for air and dying every time I closed my eyes. Guilt consumed me to no end. I felt like I was to blame, because after all it was me who introduced him to cocaine, and it was me who knew the spot to go to, to get our next fix.

Word had gotten back to me that it was Pinky who ordered the hit on George. His homeboys by the names of Tricky C, Scarface, Ghetto, and Insane were all in the car that pulled up and killed my cousin. To make it even worse, they were Gersons, part of a much-known rival gang that we were always beefing with. They were trying to make a name for themselves, but instead, this caused another war. I went on a rampage. I burned Pinky's house to the ground by throwing burning cocktails into it, as well as robbed and shot up his other drug houses. I vowed within myself that I would make them all pay. My footprints in the street were being made all over the place. I was more vicious and worse than I had ever been. Spreading more fear, demanding more respect while having plenty of money and plenty of access to guns and drugs. I found out that there was a Gerson member who went by the name of Butterball secretly living in my neighborhood, so I sent one of my little homeboys, G Rodd, to go shoot him and make a statement that they couldn't be here in our neighborhood. Butterball was a bit more experienced than G Rodd though and before G Rodd could pull the trigger, he shot G Rodd, severely injuring him. The police wanted G Rodd to press charges but it was my order that he would not cooperate with them. We would handle court in the street and deal with the situation on our own terms. I remember thinking to myself, "If you want something done right, you better do it yourself." So, I went looking for Butterball over the course of a few days. He showed up at night, trying to move some things out of his house, trying to remain under the radar. I approached him quietly from behind and tapped him. When he turned around, I pressed my gun into his stomach and said, "You've met your match buddy." I pulled the trigger and Butterball collapsed. His girlfriend began to scream, "Please! Please! Why are you doing this!?" I think God was involved that night because instead of shooting her as well, I ran off into the darkness.

For months, I went into hiding, yet was still doing dirt. The war on the streets continued to escalate so bad that gang leaders and Las Vegas politicians were on the radio asking for peace, and wanted to start a truce. A peace festival was held at Lorenzi Park where all the gang leaders from the West Side would come together in attempt to end the war. I was furious that the guys who killed my cousin were still alive so since all the gangs from the West Side had come together, I contacted surrounding gangs from North Town to join us in avenging George's death.

CHAPTER 7

Laurence Weekly and Greg Atkins were some of the main promoters in this peace treaty. Laurence was one of the good guys. He was very educated and a community leader. He'd often put together programs for the youth to keep kids off the streets and out of gangs. Years later he would become the city councilman and work as an assistant to Mayor Oscar Goodman. Although the West Side had come together in hopes of peace there was lots of bloodshed in the street. I hated the Bloods and I hated the Gersons, with great prejudice and passion. So of course, I did everything I could to make my presence feared among those gangs. With the West Side Las Vegas gangs being larger than us, we always had to come hard and demand respect, making sure that we were revered in the street. Now all the gangs from North Las Vegas were joining together in what we called The North Town Family. There were thousands of us. We took over and shut down every neighborhood on the West Side. Everyday you'd turn on the TV and hear a report about someone getting shot or killed on the West Side. Although this was short lived, it only lasted about the span of three months.

This was also during a time that one of my girlfriends, Tammy, was also pregnant. She paged me one night to inform me that she was going into labor. I didn't know what to say or do. This was during a night that I had just shot someone from the Gerson gang. I told my homeboys to drop me off at the hospital. I remember while she was in labor about to give birth, I paced back and forth. I had a long trench coat and inside it I had three guns. I remember people were asking me if I felt comfortable enough to take my coat off but because my guns were so big, I refused. I thought that anyone who walked through the door could possibly be the police coming to get me. That night I saw my son born into this world; C'Tory Mathews. However, I was so high and numb from the anger that was inside of me, I couldn't feel the excitement. Needless to say, as I watched the news in the morning, I saw the person who had gotten shot remained alive. It was as if God was only letting me go so far. I don't know how that guy lived. It could've only been Gods intervention for him. That guy had been shot several times.

Two days after my son was born, my friends and I chased a guy down an alley to gun him down. We all aimed and began shooting, only my gun did not go off. It was jammed up that night. I began to think that God was dealing with me. None of my plans were going through. I was high out of my mind and I began to be paranoid, even to the point where I thought my friends were plotting against me. I remember riding in the car that night with my friends wondering if they were going to kill me because my gun did not go off. Inside, I was very much afraid. You see, the way the gang life was, we all did dirt, and if one of us did not include ourselves in certain dirty things, then we were found untrustworthy. Even though it was just one incident where my gun was jammed up and would not shoot, I couldn't trust what my friends were thinking. So, in my heart, I prepared myself for a moment that never came. I should've been dead. However, not one word was ever said. My friends and I went on with our normal everyday routines. I did not like the feeling of being paranoid, so I stopped doing the drugs and set my focus on the war at hand. Also, due to the street wars, Tammy's house had been shot up on occasions because my enemies often looked for me. Though no one was ever shot, my lifestyle only kept me from being around her. Since it was unsafe for me to be around her or my son, we were never able to form a real bond until years later.

Through it all, Alicia and I were going in opposite directions in our relationship. Everything began to go in a downward spiral for me, and I turned back to drugs and alcohol. It had been months since I had gotten high and no doubt, here were the same paranoid thoughts again; my friends were out to get me and plotting to kill me. I didn't want to show weakness. I remember in a meeting one day asking my best friend at the time, who was also one of the most notorious Crips in North Town, if he had plans to kill me. Of course, I had my hand on my weapon planning for the worst. He assured me that night that my mind was going places they shouldn't have been going. However, my drug habit had now gotten to the point where it was the worst in my life. I could no longer think straight. I didn't want to be around anyone, so I stayed away. For weeks at a time no one heard from me. I was no longer myself. To make matters worse, my one time best friend, Clinky, had gotten killed, and everyone pointed the finger at me. They assumed that I had killed my friend because people were hearing stories about me robbing him for his drugs and money. As angry as I've ever been at Clinky, I don't think I could've ever come to a place in my mind where I could be responsible for his death. After all, we grew up as best friends. So, at this point, all I cared about was my next high.

I soon became homeless for a while. I would break into abounded houses just to sleep and keep out of the cold. On some of the warmer days, I'd go into the Motel 6 pool area and go to sleep on the lawn chairs. One time I remember breaking into the back of an empty U-Haul truck and sleeping for a few hours. Sometimes I just wanted to commit a stupid crime and allow myself to get caught by the police so I could go to jail and have a bed and some food. At the most random moment, I ran into a guy on the street. He was white and wore plain clothes; nothing spectacular. He said he could sense that I was in the slums. I thought of course with my lack of rest; my eyes were bloodshot and I smelt like liquor. But he took the opportunity to do Gods work and he said, "Hey man, no matter what you do, ALWAYS keep God with you. He'll never leave you. God will forgive you for the worst things you've ever done." I was numb at first, and the words he spoke did not affect me until months later. Sometimes I would visit my mother, hoping that maybe I could live with her again, but this wasn't happening. My mother and stepfather could not even trust me. So, I never stayed long. Sometimes I would just go there and they wouldn't even know, just to have some peace and quiet until one day I found one of my old guns hidden in my mom's house. That day, I robbed someone off the street for $150. I used the money to buy drugs and a $30 hotel room.

After cleaning myself up I went to the strip club and tried to persuade young ladies to let me stay the night with them. One of the young ladies ended up giving me money and let me stay at her place for a while. She gave me enough money every day to support my drug habit. Things were fine until I got high one night and went to the strip club she worked. I had done so much cocaine and was paranoid out of my mind. My heart was palpitating. I was very uncomfortable, so I just left. My eyes were blinded as I went outside only for the sun to be coming up. When I got back to her house, I made her feel uncomfortable. She wanted to start an argument. Normally I would've turned violent, but I was so high I just turned around and left. I took her car and drove off. I went to a pay phone and gave my partner, Bushwick, a call.

Years prior my mother had adopted Bushwick. We called him that because he was a short person, kind of like the midget rapper from the Ghetto Boys. Bushwick was always down for whatever. He loved to get into a brawl. He was one person I could count on if I was to get into a fight with one of my enemies. My mother loved him as if he were her own son. She helped him graduate high school. Bushwick was very athletic. He could play any kind of sport, but his favorite was wrestling. He even had an opportunity to go to college. However, when my older friends and I would come around, my mom would get so angry with us. She thought we were a very bad influence on Bushwick. Though Bushwick and I were the same age, I would pick him up from time to time from high school. I remember the police pulled me over and harassed me one day picking him up from school. Bushwick and I were 17 years old at the time. The cops put us both in handcuffs, sat him down in an ant hill and made him watch while they roughed me up. Bushwick was screaming because the ants were crawling all over him and biting him. Bushwick and I had been through so much together.

So now, a couple years later this day I had given him a call after leaving this girl's house. I just needed somewhere to calm down and relax for a moment. Bushwick suggested that I needed some weed to help me relax so we headed to a popular weed spot. I remember pulling up; it was a Sunday morning. Right next to the place they were selling weed, I saw a small house church called Grace Temple. They had service going on and just out front, I noticed my dad's truck parked outside along the sidewalk. I knew my dad had gotten out of prison and I had heard rumors of him turning his life around. While in prison he had been baptized, and gave his life to the Lord. So, I went into the church to see him.

I was so strung out on drugs. I was only there to get weed, but it was no accident that I ended up in the church. There were only about twenty members or so, and as soon as I walked in the preacher stopped preaching. Everyone all turned around and stared dead at me. They say come as you are, and I was every bit of a demonic gang member. My eyes were bloodshot red and I reeked of liquor and drugs. The minister said, "God bless your young man, God bless you. Your times are about to change." Then I saw my dad. Tears filled his eyes; he didn't say one word. He practically ran down the aisle and gave me a huge hug. It was the hug I always wanted from him.

CHAPTER 8

I knew with that hug it was God. And with that hug I felt love from my dad for the very first time. Love conquers all fears, doubts, and worries. Every burden and every depressing or dark emotion I had built up over the years were lifted off me like a ton of bricks. I just cried; my dad's hug was so uplifting. At that very moment I became a firm believer that God gave me the ability to forgive my dad without a single grudge. It was the same man that I hated with a passion and for many years, would like to have killed. But I could let the past be in the past and I felt light as a feather; like a new person.

It was a monumental moment in my life, and though I was catapulted to another place in my mind, I was not ready to surrender unto the Lord. The purpose, however, was God allowing me to begin a father/son relationship with my dad that we never had. In the past, it was always about drugs or money but from that point on, we had a real relationship. We would go to various restaurants all the time and just talk for hours. The more we talked, the more we realized we were so much alike. At this point in my life I witnessed my dad as a totally different person. He was the caretaker of an elderly woman who was very sick and couldn't get around on her own. My dad would cook and clean for her. My dad gave happiness and peace to the lady during her last days on earth so that she wouldn't struggle. I really admired that about him. I was still homeless however, so the moments I had with him were uplifting. To survive though, I continued to rob people, whether it was to eat or have a place to sleep. Sex, drugs, money and violence all possessed my mind and had a strong grip on my heart. Living in those circumstances, I was so miserable and I was never satisfied. No matter what, Satan continued after me constantly.

Being around my dad or anyone else, I manipulated my appearance and kept myself up so no one could see how bad I really was. However, my dad was one person who could see through it all. One night, things got a little out of hand as I partied and did lots of cocaine and drank hard liquor all night long. Not having much sleep, I became so paranoid that I believed once again that my friends were out to kill me, so I went into hiding for another four or five days. During that time, I didn't see my dad much. I felt like I needed to see him. It was as if it was an opportunity for me to escape, so I went to visit him. I felt he was the only person I could trust and let my guard down. I went to the elderly woman's house where my dad was staying and began to knock on the door. A moment later he opened the door to me, and I collapsed in his arms. I knew I reeked with liquor and cocaine, oozing from my pores. He just carried me to his room, laid me into his bed and tucked me in like a little child. I slept for days. I would often hear my dad praying for me. One day I had strength enough to wake up to the smell of eggs and toast as my dad made me breakfast and served me in the bed. I was starving so I ate it in seconds. Afterwards, I felt so much better. As my dad sat beside me, he said to me, "Son, I know what you are going through. I've been through the same battle." He asked me if I was willing to ween myself off drugs. I said, "Yes, absolutely." So, for the next couple of weeks, I did not leave my dad's room. I remember there was a Bible on the nightstand that my dad would read constantly. At this point, I had never read the Bible but everything now seemed so different in my mind. I began to talk to the Lord in prayer. My dad and I fellowshipped together, and I really loved it.

After I felt better, I decided to get out of the house and get some fresh air. I felt it was time for me to get on my feet and support myself. However, my past had caught up with me and I was arrested for the attempted murder of Butterball. While I was in jail, I found out that there were some Gerson leaders in the same module as myself. They were terrified of my presence; so, afraid that they went into protective custody. Days later they sent a message to me, that they didn't have anything to do with George's death and didn't want any trouble with me. My first thought was to disregard the message but then I began to reason with myself. I felt like this could be an opportunity for me to begin changing my life, so I replied to him saying what happened to my cousin was out of my hands. I let him know that as far as I was concerned, we no longer had to be enemies but the rest of the gang would have to determine for themselves what they wanted to do. He agreed and in doing so, he called up his friend, Lakara, who was the only witness as well as the one to press charges. He convinced her not to come to court, so they had no reason to keep me. They had no weapon and no witness, so I was released on my own recognizance.

When I was released from jail, I knew that my days on the street were numbered. Word had gotten around that I had made a truce with a couple of Gersons and it angered my friends. They were even spreading rumors supposing that I had snitched to get out, so now everyone seemed to be against me. The truth was that I was just simply tired. I hated being paranoid. I felt like I was always in some form of danger, whether it be from my own homeboys or from actual enemies that I had accumulated over the years. So, at this point, all I wanted to do was make enough money to get out of dodge. I began to hang out on the strip. Anyone who knows Las Vegas knows that the Las Vegas strip was famous for having some of the best prostitutes in the world, so I figured I would attract some of the finest women and manipulate them into making me rich. I was broke as a joke, but my game was strong and I dressed like a millionaire. I used my gift to smooth talk women and persuade them. I'd pick up a girl here and there, but nothing became serious, until one day I was hanging out with a friend of mine who was a big-time pimp named Spencer. He said to me, "You know there's a girl who's been looking at you and only you. You've got plenty of action. Guys from all over the country have been trying to get this girl, but her eyes are on you."

CHAPTER 9

Days had gone by and every night in the same spot, at the same time I would look up to see this girl staring at me from the bar. It was as if she knew I was going to be there, and I sure knew she was going to be there, so I made it a point to be there every night. Sure, enough she would sit there just twirling her hair and staring at me for long periods of time. Every night I would send her a message with complete confidence. Some days I would write my number on a napkin and walk by her and drop it, expecting her to pick it up and call me the next day. Other times I would pay the bartender to give her a message for me. She would never give me the time of day though. She never responded to any of my words. She'd act like she didn't even hear me, but I knew that I had to be consistent, and I knew that even though she ignored me, she had eyes for me. In the meantime, however, I was only twenty years old, hanging out at the Caesars Palace and drinking champagne with a new circle of friends. Hanging out with these guys made me want to do better. I was infatuated with their lifestyle, and it motivated me. They drove Ferraris and Rolls-Royces, and had nothing short of the best things money could buy. It was the lifestyle that I had been chasing. Up until now, I had been going about it all the wrong way. These guys didn't care about guns or violence. All they cared about was women, money and possessions. It may have been a blessing for me to go from being a violent gang member to a smooth talking con man, always looking for the ladies because the death tolls continued to rise. Anthony Glen, a guy who I looked up to growing up, was also found dead. The death of those close to me was never something I could get used to. I had lots of pain in my heart. I was constantly confronted with the thought, "What if it was me?" I should've died so many times in those streets.

Everything was going well until one day while I was in the Caesars Palace at the lounge drinking champagne with Spencer. Suddenly I heard, "Are you Cory Mathews?" I turned around and hear they were; the FBI. Usually, I would have avoided them at all cost and by any means necessary but because it had been only a few short weeks since I had been out of jail, I figured I had nothing to hide and no reason to resist. I thought maybe it was because I was a twenty-year-old minor, not old enough to be in the casino let alone drinking. So, I said to the officer, "Yes, I'm Cory Mathews." They immediately handcuffed me and took me to the county jail. It turns out that they only wanted to question me about some murders that had taken place in North Las Vegas. I told them that I had no clue what they were talking about. I even said to the police that I was in fear for my own life and didn't hang out with my friends any longer. Therefore, since I didn't cooperate with them in giving them the information they sought, they brought up old warrants from traffic violations, and charged me for being underage, drinking in a bar. So now, I am stuck in jail with a five-thousand-dollar cash bond and no possible way to pay it. I called my mom to tell her what was going on. She responded and told me that there was some woman named Jackie trying to get a hold of me, wanting to help me out. I didn't know who the woman was, but next thing I know, my bail was paid in full and I was released from jail. Late that afternoon I walked out of the county jail to a limousine waiting for me. The driver took me to the Alexis Park Resort and checked me in where I was given an apartment suite. When I walked in I found a note on the bed that said, "You have a new wardrobe, weed and just about everything else you need. P.S. See you in the morning."

Just like that, overnight my life changed. I walked into the closet and there were all kinds of very expensive high end suits and alligator shoes to match each one. I also had brand new underwear and socks. The refrigerator was full of champagne and orange juice, and I had the best weed money could buy. There was also a paper bag on a dresser with twenty thousand dollars wrapped up in a rubber band inside. So, I rolled a joint, got in the Jacuzzi and enjoyed myself for the night. I felt like a king. Early the next morning, in walks Jackie. To my surprise, it was the very same woman I had been trying to pick up at the bar for the past month or so. When I was sending her messages through the bartender I had given her my mom's number as a sure means of contact. Little did I know, she kept it. Here she was handing me seven thousand dollars, a Rolex watch and seventy thousand dollars' worth of casino chips. This was her way of choosing me, even though the watch and the chips were stolen just hours before. I quickly took them and cashed them in and I kept the Rolex for myself. For the next few months she was what I called my bottom. Every morning was like Christmas. She would give me money and gifts, and every night I celebrated as if it were New Year's Eve. I bought my first sixty-thousand-dollar car and lived life like a celebrity. On various occasions, she'd come home with forty thousand dollars here or ninety thousand there. She never came home with anything less than a thousand dollars a night. She'd also bring home expensive watches and jewelry. One time she even came home with some kind of real expensive telescope. Jackie was a master thief; no ordinary prostitute. She'd get her guys drunk or put them to sleep by giving them a good massage. She'd find ways to steal everything the guys had.

However, as amazing as it all seemed, it turns out before Jackie was with me, she was with another pimp named Bruce. He had nine women working for him. He had a million-dollar home in Las Vegas and a very lavish apartment in New Jersey. Jackie used to be his number one girl. She had brought Bruce over half a million dollars over the course of a few months, so it's easy to imagine why every pimp in the country wanted Jackie on their team. Yet here I am, a young gangster fresh in the game who came from nowhere and I had taken Jackie from Bruce. I was the talk of the town. In fact, every pimp and hoe in the country had my name in their mouth. What I didn't know was that the casinos that Jackie had worked out of had footage of Jackie wearing different wigs with many different guys who had reported hundreds of thousands of dollars stolen from them. So therefore, she was being investigated by the vice. One night when I was hanging out with my friends, these filmmakers by the name of the Hughes brothers who made movies like Menace To Society and Dead Presidents approached us about wanting to do a film documentary about the life of a pimp. The majority of us turned them down, for the lifestyle and the means of income that we were about were still against the law. Yet a few of my friends, pimps known as Gorgeous Dre, Charm, and Kenny Red just to name a few, all simultaneously agreed to do the movie. When the film was released, all hell broke loose for every pimp living in Las Vegas. The Las Vegas sting operation was in full effect. They even used the film to build their case. So most of us took our girls and went elsewhere throughout the country to get away. Most of my friends had it made financially, so they were ok. As for me, I stayed in Las Vegas under the radar.

CHAPTER 10

The year was now 1997 and Mike Tyson and Evander Holyfield were scheduled to fight their second fight. Being a much-anticipated fight, every pimp in the nation had their game out to make money. While our girls were out getting money for us, we were going to the fight. In the MGM Grand that night, lots of celebrities, high rollers, pimps and prostitutes were all out and about. People came from all over the world to have a good time in Las Vegas. Being that this was such a big night for everyone, my friends and I decided to have a good time before the fight started, so we began to snort cocaine and have a few drinks to start the night off. Jackie had gone out and to the Bally's Hotel and Casino where she turned a few tricks and ended up meeting a professional gambler. During this time, my friends and I were getting high waiting to go into the fight to watch Tyson and Holyfield. It was then that I got a page from Jackie. She needed to see me ASAP. I was automatically concerned that something had happened to my money, so she calmed me down and said I wouldn't be disappointed. We meet in the parking garage of the MGM and she hands me a duffle bag filled with $150,000 cash with a request that we leave town. I agreed but in the meantime, for the rest of that night, we celebrated and partied.

As planned, the next morning Jackie and I moved to Hollywood, California. Things were going well; she worked the escort service in the day and walked up and down Sunset Boulevard during the night, getting in and out of cars, turning trick after trick. I'd fly back to Las Vegas periodically to visit my family, but eventually wanted to expand my experience and go to different places around the country. So, we packed up and moved to Phoenix, Arizona, where it all turned out to be one bad experience after the other. My girls would often go to jail and I ended up wrecking my car. Among many other small things that caused a great deal of frustration, money was slow. So, Phoenix left me with a bad taste in my mouth as we packed up and moved to Atlantic City.

Atlantic City was a town much like Las Vegas. We weren't there long because I had lots of girls that were working in Philadelphia, so I traveled between the two cities weekly. A convention was being held one time at Foxwoods Casino in

Connecticut, so I decided to send my girls there to make some money over the weekend. While they were there, I hung out in Rhode Island where my friend, Cook, and I stayed in a cheap hotel. Next door to the hotel was a topless nightclub, so we went into the nightclub after unpacking to have a couple of drinks and relax. We ordered a couple of bottles of champagne and sat down. Within five minutes, the owner of the club approached us and asked, "Are you guys pimps?" This was such a weird experience for me because in Las Vegas, pimps weren't very welcome in strip clubs. Although it was obvious that we were pimps, I didn't know whether to say yes or no. I mean, I smelled good, had a fresh perm, had a red and black suit with red alligator shoes, and diamond framed glasses on my face. So instead of saying yes or no, I asked the man why he questioned. I said, "We're but merely in the entertainment business, and just here to have a good time." He then responded to me that he wanted to welcome us into his club and was happy to have us being that not many limos are ever seen in that town. So, we were treated as celebrities. He sent two of his best dancers over just for us. Throughout the night, I had a conversation with one of the girls who, after hearing we were from Las Vegas, wanted to go with us. I told the girl that if she could come up with enough ones, she could come all over the world with me. She gave me fifteen thousand dollars and said she wanted to be mine.

After the weekend was over, the girls and I went back to Atlantic City. The young girl from Rhode Island did not last very long in my household. She had gotten arrested the second night that I sent her out and it scared her. The other women in my household, especially Jackie, treated her harsh and didn't make it easy for her to fit in. She did not want this lifestyle, so she went back to where she came from. She didn't make very much money so I didn't care. All I really ever cared about was money. After a while, the money flow wasn't as good for us in Atlantic City. The girls would have hard times bringing me money. It went from thousands of dollars a night to just low hundreds, so when the money began to trickle and get low, I decided to pack up. We left Atlantic City and went to Boston, Massachusetts. While in Boston, during the day my girls worked the escort service, and by night, we'd hang out in a place called China Town where all the hookers would go and get in and out of cars with guy after guy. The money was decent in Boston, so I

41

decided to stay. Every other night the police would come through in a paddy wagon with sirens blaring, rounding up all the prostitutes and taking them to jail for a night. Girls would often run from the paddy wagon because for the average night's work, you'd make anywhere from five hundred to one thousand dollars. However, if you went to jail, your bail was two hundred dollars, so the whole night's work could go down the drain. Most of the girls had warrants, so this became a routine game of cat and mouse when the police came through.

I have lots of memories from my days in Boston, some of which were funny. For instance, one night, hanging out with my friends I stepped off to the side to talk to this girl. She was what you called a renegade. This meant that she was out prostituting without a pimp. Lots of pimps gave her a hard time because she wouldn't choose. While I was talking to her, the paddy wagon came out of nowhere and attempted to gather up all the girls, so she took off like a bolt of lightning to get away. My friend and I ran with her. We ran through rat infested streets and ended up hiding in a parking lot from the police. It was a very nasty area, littered with used condoms, dirty needles, busted crack pipes, and other drug paraphernalia. The girl was hiding under a car with nothing on but a bra, g string and high heels. The police that were chasing us began to shine bright lights and look between cars to find us. The cops saw my friend and me while we were ducking in front of a parked car. They told us to freeze and as they searched us they asked us repeatedly why we were there hiding, and where the drugs were. The honest truth of the matter was I was only there because I wanted the girl to choose me to be her pimp, but I couldn't tell the police that. So, I told them we were looking for dates. They didn't believe me. They threatened to take us to jail if we didn't tell them the truth, so not wanting to go to jail, I came up with the story of a lifetime. I told the police that my friend was giving me oral sex and we were hiding so no one would find us. It sounded so bizarre the girl underneath the car could not help but to start laughing while my friend was looking at me with the look of straight embarrassment. He couldn't believe that I said that but everyone was laughing so loud that the cops did not arrest us. Instead, they gave us a warning and let us go.

After a few weeks in Boston, I didn't really like it. My girls were always being arrested and I constantly had to bail them out. At one point, one of my girls had gone missing. A whole week had gone by; Jackie had called all the hospitals and jails every day to see if she would turn up. We were all worried and concerned until one night, I spotted her getting in and out of cars. I knew that a date would only last about five to ten minutes, so I stuck around and waited. When her date ended and she was getting out of the car, I approached her and confronted her. I told her she had better give me all my money. She reached in her bra, pulled out four hundred dollars and handed it to me. I told her she had a lot more work to do, so get me the rest of my money. Later, that night, while a bunch of us limos were standing outside on the sidewalk, talking amongst ourselves, drinking Cognac and smoking weed, a car comes speeding down the road and almost drives onto the sidewalk where we were standing, as if someone was going to run us over. We all jumped out of the way, and I can remember cussing because I spilled Cognac on my suit. A group of guys came out of the car and aimed their guns at me. I must admit, though I had never been scared, I sure was this night. I figured it was all over for me and that all the bad stuff I'd done in my past had finally came back to haunt me. Usually in these situations I could fast talk my way out of anything but this time, the more I talked, I only made matters worse. The group of youngsters were becoming very irritated with me. They wanted me to know they meant business, that I was in their city and the girl belonged to them now. By this time, a large group of my friends, pimps, corralled around, letting me know they had my back. I told the young guys they could have the girl, and that I was not willing to die over her. We were all blessed that no shots were fired and no one was injured. The group of youngsters went their way and we went ours. Apparently, this was a big problem in Boston, in which the young thugs would often kidnap prostitutes and make them work for them. This was all the more reason for me to leave. I had been in enough drama my whole life and did not want to welcome anymore. We decided to stay there for Christmas, when my girls surprised me with a hand-crafted cane with a beautiful woman carved in one side of the handle and an angel on the other side. My name was embedded with diamonds around the handle. This cane also turned into a knife when I pulled the handle out of the shaft. I took the cane everywhere I went from that point on.

Not long after that, we went back to California and things began to look good for me. I had plenty of money and what I considered four of the best working girls in the country on my team. A friend of mine named Kyle who designed websites for underground escort services to promote girls came to me with an idea. He said he was going to Japan and opening up a massage parlor/night and strip club. In his mind, if we took some of our American girls to Japan, we could make a fortune, live legit and wash our money. Of course, I loved the idea. We decided to put our plan together and make this happen. During this period, I got a call from Las Vegas; it was my stepfather. He told me that my mother was very sick; all the years my mother was abused by my biological father, in addition to all the stress and weight that she carried as I lived in the streets, with her wondering daily whether I was alive. My enemies, whether it be gangsters or crooked police, didn't just threaten me but they threatened my mother from time to time. The police would often kick in the door to her home and threaten her, supposing she would tell them where I was. They always put guns to my mom's head, my stepfathers head, and even my baby sister's. This had all taken its toll upon her. This caused my mother to have a nervous breakdown, during which time she had not recovered, but only gotten worse. So, she was admitted into a mental hospital. After getting the news of my mother being sick, I knew I had to go back to Vegas.

I was 22 years old and it was a miracle that I was still living. I had traveled all over the country and had a $70,000 Cadillac DTS and a Range Rover. My bottom girls drove Mercedes. I was no longer a gang member, I was no longer homeless, and I was no longer sick on drugs, though I did do social drugs. Everything had boiled down to me just wanting to be there for my family. So, I left a few girls in Hollywood to work the escort service and continue my operations. Jackie and I flew out to Las Vegas as fast as we could. When we got to Vegas, the detectives had been patiently waiting for us and we we're both arrested and at a $50,000 cash bond. So of course, I put up the $50,000 cash and we were both bailed out the next day. We retained an attorney by the name of John Turco. The police had years of investigation and all kinds of footage of Jackie leaving hotel rooms and stealing money. The only thing they could charge me with initially was living off the earnings of a prostitute. They also found one of the watches Jackie had stolen and a small bag of cocaine. In order for the drug charge to stick, they needed Jackie to testify against me and say that I was her pimp. I really admired Jackie because she could've told on me but never did. We fought our cases for a year and a half. Jackie was sentenced to five years in prison. I also was sentenced to five years, but only with a suspended sentence, which meant probation with restitution and large fines. My cars, houses and jewelry were all seized.

CHAPTER 11

Once again, I was able to avoid prison walls and jail cells. Even though I was on probation, I was basically free. I used some jewelry that I had hid at my mom's house to make my way back on top in the streets. I contacted a friend of mine, Juilian. This was the guy who got houses for pimps and drug dealers. It was easy for us to have cash but we never had credit and we were unable to put things in our own names. So Juilian would find ways to get us new identities, with social security numbers, W2s and a line of credit. This made it able for us to take large sums of cash to him and in turn, buy cars, houses; pretty much whatever we wanted. Since my main girl, Jackie, was doing time, I had another girl whose name was Tahony. I liked Tahony because she knew how to hustle. She had been with a couple of young pimps before, however I could groom her into the way I wanted her to be. She was to be recognized internationally as I was. When I first met her, I promised that I would make her into a superstar and asked her to come to Hollywood with me, and she said yes. So, with my mom doing better now, I could take her to Hollywood with me and show her the ropes. I put her to work on Sunset Boulevard. Though I still had three other girls working for me, she soon became my main girl.

The year was 1999 and a big convention called the Comdex was in Las Vegas. People from all over would come there, especially pimps and prostitutes, so back to Vegas we went. The four women could clean house. We made lots of money that weekend. So, I treated all the girls and took them shopping. Everyone got their hair and nails done, and on that Sunday afternoon we went to eat at a restaurant called H&H BBQ. Every now and then you might find a famous person or some celebrity going there to taste some good ole BBQ. Usually when I went there, they treated me like I was a celebrity, so naturally it became one of my favorite places to eat. However, this particular Sunday there were a lot of church members that were there for lunch. The service was horrible that day. Forty-five minutes had gone by and the waiter never came to the table to take our order. So just as we were about to leave, almost angry, an older lady dressed in all white in the booth next to us asked me, "What do you do for a living?" I said, "I am a business man in the entertainment business." She said, "I can

46

see that you are very successful." Of course, I was dressed to impress. I had lots of jewelry on and a Mercedes outside. So, I replied, "I am very blessed, the Lord has been good to me." She said, "Oh yes, the Lord has shown you mercy." So, I asked her what she did for a living. She replied, "I am an ambulance driver." I said, "Now that's a real job; your job is really important. You help people and save their lives." She said, "Yes I do, and I've come here today to take you to the hospital." I said, "What? I'm not sick, I don't need to go to the hospital." And she said, "Well, your father says it's time to come home." I knew instantaneously exactly what she was talking about. It brought tears to my eyes as she began to speak prophetically of my former days and the days to come. She told me that my days were numbered as a free man, and that I couldn't run from the law any longer. She said that God was going to shut down my operation and the best thing for me to do was to turn myself in. Tahony and the girls did not understand what was going on. They had never seen me in such an emotional state. The lady soon turned to them and told them that they had to stop listening to me, and if they didn't they would end up in jail as well. At this point, I was about to lose it. I took my girls and began to leave as I felt the woman had overstepped her boundaries. She followed us outside and apologized, and she invited us to her church. The ride home was the most awkward ride we could ever have had. None of us spoke a word, nor was there any music playing in the car. I knew that what the woman had said had the girls thinking. When we got home, I wanted to be left alone, so I spent time in my study just thinking about what the woman had said.

As it seemed, everything the woman said came to pass. All the girls were arrested the next day except for Tahony. She and I went to a party at my friend, Gregory Peck's, house where there were lots of drugs. We hung out at the party for a while, we had a couple of drinks and a friend of mine had given me a dollar bill that was folded up with cocaine inside of it. So Tahony and I went outside to be alone. We sat in the car and just as I was about to take a snort of cocaine, the police shined lights in my window. I had no idea they were watching his house. We just so happened to be in the wrong place at the wrong time. They asked me all sorts of questions and I gave them my identification, which was someone else's name that Juilian had given me. As they ran my name in the system,

47

nothing was coming up but for reason of suspicion and the dollar bill filled with cocaine, they took me to jail. When I got to the county they scanned my fingerprints and that's when they could find out my true identity. I was charged with possession of a controlled substance and violation of probation. I had no bail, so there was no way I could get out. Because my probation was a suspended sentence, I now looked forward to doing a forty-two-month sentence in prison. While I was waiting for my sentencing, my attorney informed me that he was going to try to get my court date postponed. I didn't ask questions as to why; I just let it be. All I knew was as soon as I got to the prison yard, I had a line of enemies that were waiting to kill me, but on the bright side, I had just as long of a line of loved ones who would jump to my aid and have my back. It didn't matter though; I felt closer to death than I ever had in my entire life.

During this time while I was awaiting my sentencing in the county jail, weeks had gone by. I stayed to myself mostly. One night while I slept, I dreamt and saw my whole life from the beginning. I also saw a horrifying end. I heard a voice in my dream that said, "Repent! Your end shall come quickly!" I woke up terrified. Days later I had the same dream with the same voice; however, being honest with myself, I wasn't ready to repent. My heart was still festering with lots of anger and even though I was going to prison, I was still very greedy and lustful. Either one of two things were going to happen as far as I was concerned. I was going to die in prison or get released back to the streets in about forty-two months. I still had three faithful women out there stacking money for me. So, I was, in my mind, far from repentance. A few more days passed and I had the same exact dream, only this time the voice said, "If you repent and receive Jesus, God will give something better than you've ever had." When I woke from the dream, I knew in my heart what God was going to give me; love! A wife and a family full of love! I began to soften up inside as God in his own way continued to deal with me. It got so serious and intense over the course of the week that I couldn't deny God any longer. I said, "Yes Lord! I repent!" I took advantage of my time, and I did lots of reading and studying.

From that moment on, I stopped responding to any letters and didn't except any more visitors from the women I had. There was a guy named Greg Grey who was also in the county jail for a long list of charges. Greg was a former bail bondsman. He was responsible for helping all the big-time pimps, drug dealers, and gang members get bonded out of jail. He did lots of crooked things in the aid of helping most of us criminals. Now his criminal activities had caught up with him, which he found himself finding his own case in a county jail as well. However, Greg had turned his life around during his experience in jail, and gave his life to the Lord. He had lots of influence in the county jail and many people would sit down with him as he would hold a daily Bible study. He approached me one day about joining him for Bible study and possibly becoming a prayer partner with him. Greg and I were already friends, so it was easy for me to say yes and join him in Bible study and prayer. We prayed daily for people and our Bible study group had grown tremendously. People were in there for murders, kidnappings, robberies, and all kinds of crime, yet they were giving their lives to the Lord on a daily basis. I saw murders with tears in their eyes, and rival gang members becoming friends. It was very powerful to me.

Every now and then Greg would have a seizure during the night hours which grew worse and worse each time. So, we held fasting and prayers, hoping to see him healed and doing better. The day before my sentencing, Greg and I had a discussion. He asked me to promise him that if I were to ever get out, I wouldn't come back. I said, "I promise you." Later that night, Greg had another seizure, yet he did not make it. He died that night. And while none of us in the module really knew what was going on, the guards came and got me early in the morning, put shackles on me and took me to court. They informed me of Greg's death. My heart sank into my stomach, and my eyes filled with tears. Sadness had begun to overtake me, yet I thought to myself that Greg was in a great place with God. His faith was strong, and I knew that Jesus was his Lord.

So, I continued the day and went to court. When the judge called my name, my attorney asked if he could approach the bench. So, my attorney, my probation officer and the district attorney approached the bench to talk to the judge. They whispered amongst themselves for a few minutes, then everyone returned to their respectable places. The judge asked me if I wanted to take the plea bargain they were offering, and before I could speak my attorney said, "Tell them yes." The plea bargain was for a dishonorable discharge, with fine and restitution. This meant that I could never get in trouble again. If I did so happen to go back to jail, I would never be eligible for any parole or probation. I asked the judge, "Does this mean I can go home?" The judge replied, "Yes." I told the judge he would never see my face again under those circumstances. So, remembering my promise to Greg, yet with a saddened heart, I saw this as another miracle. Here we are once again, and I am free. This time, with no probation, no house arrest, not even a warrant.

CHAPTER 12

As soon as I got out, I went to a little church called Prayer Center Revival. I said within myself, "I can't fight God any longer." So, with great zeal, I surrendered my life to Jesus Christ. I sat and learned under the man who became my spiritual father. His name is Prince Davis. He taught and he preached with such power. It seemed as if God would speak through him every day, to my circumstance. God was blessing me, and I wanted everybody to have this same experience. So, I often brought my old friends from the neighborhood to church and I told as many people as I could about my experience with Jesus. Even though my life had changed and I was definitely a new man, the fact still remained that I had these very large fines and restitution I had to pay. I needed to get a job, but because of my record and my lack of experience no one would hire me. So, I furthered my education and went and got my GED. Soon after, a deacon from the church named Thomas Coleman who knew someone who worked in human resources at Walmart asked me if I would like to work at Walmart because he could get me a job there. I said absolutely. So, I went and filled out an application, and did what was required of me to get the job. They hired me as a maintenance man. My job was to clean floors, take the trash out, and clean the toilets and the bathrooms. Ironically, it was this same Wal-Mart that I used to go to try to pick up women. And now, I was picking up trash. This made me think God must surely have a sense of humor. One thing I do know for sure is that God had sent me there to teach me a life lesson that could not be learned in school or seminary, and to prepare me for the next level of ministry.

This was a drastic change from living the superstar lifestyle, what I thought to be the American Dream. I went from having hundreds of thousands of dollars to working for just above minimum wage, making only $7.25 an hour. I no longer had long pretty hair and fancy clothes and jewelry, but a bald head, some dingy slacks and religious t-shirts. To pass time, I'd read my Bible on my breaks. One day as I was taking out the garbage, I heard someone quietly whisper from behind, "Daddy! Daddy! I want you to come back home with me, and make things like how they used to be." Immediately I knew the voice and turned around. It was one of my old girls. To be honest, I was more embarrassed than anything. I only allowed women to

51

see me at my best in the past. Now I'm caught being the lowest that I could be. I replied to her and asked how she was doing. As we talked for a mere two minutes, she said she wanted me to quit my job there and come back home so she could take care of me. Talk about temptation! However, my commitment to the Lord was set in stone. I had made up in my mind that I was never going back, and I made a vow to live the rest of my life unto the Lord. She refused to accept that I was a changed man and put her card in my shirt pocket, telling me she hoped I would change my mind soon. As she walked away, I did the only thing I knew to do that was right. I ripped up her phone number and asked God to strengthen me.

Weeks had gone by and I had gotten my first raise. My supervisor had been noticing my faithfulness and hard work. He said that he'd never seen anyone be as careful and full of heart as I was. It was a very exciting moment for me, particularly because I knew God was blessing me. Over the months, I had received two more raises. Eventually, I was making $11 an hour and I was promoted to head of maintenance. Things were going great, until one day a coworker complained excessively about me reading my Bible on my breaks. The coworker also complained about me witnessing to people about Jesus. I was now an offense to her and others. Lo and behold, I was fired! I was very discouraged at first. I spoke with a friend of mine and he said that I had concrete grounds for a lawsuit against Walmart. So, I went to the EEOC (Equal Employment Opportunity Commission) to get the ball rolling and pursue the case against Walmart for religious discrimination and wrongful termination. Months had gone by and things were looking very good for me concerning the lawsuit. However, I was beginning to feel convicted about the whole thing, perhaps because my motive for suing was dollar signs. I was being sucked back into what I was delivered from. Even though I was wrongfully terminated and wanted justice, my greed was very much still alive. I did not want that. I only wanted to do what was right and be free in my conscience. So, I dropped the case and it was a great feeling!

At this point in my life, I was being blessed in my church home, and I had a new family as well. My mother and my stepfather were also faithful members of the church, and there was an amazing transformation in all of us. My pastor, Prince Davis, whom also was my spiritual father, had more influence in my life than anyone else in the world. He mentored me and even embraced me as his own son. My life had been forever changed. I was learning so much and growing so much spiritually. I was heavily involved in ministry now, and had been preaching the gospel for a span. Although I didn't have a job, I was still blessed! I lived with my mom and stepdad and I was closer to them than I had ever been. One day while I arrived early for a weekly service at the church, I was greeted in the parking lot by the police. They arrested me and took me to jail. It just so happened that I had a warrant for my arrest due to a reopening of an investigation and because I was delinquent in paying my fines because of the plea bargain I agreed to for a dishonorable discharge. I now had to face multiple judges in multiple court rooms. I called my pastor to let him know what had happened and to request prayer. I saw the hand of the Lord in this whole situation. Me being in jail turned out to be a blessing. I began holding a small Bible study in jail. People were once again giving their lives to the Lord, receiving Jesus as savior.

Weeks had gone by and one day while I was standing at the top of the tier, one of the correctional officers had stopped to talk to me. As we were talking, of course I explained to him my fair path in Christ, and how my faith had become stronger now than it had ever been. His response was that I had only a jailhouse religion and I wouldn't be there if I hadn't gotten myself in trouble. He said if I was really a child of God, I would not be there, and most likely when I got out I would go right back to the streets and right back to my old ways. At the end of this conversation, tears began to swell up in my eyes, I couldn't believe that some guy would say this. He couldn't have been any more wrong; he was so far away from the truth and that's what hurt. The truth was that I didn't do anything this time. I was merely in jail because of past issues. I went back to my cell and I prayed for hours, harder than I'd ever prayed before. "Lord set me free, and release me back to the hands of your people! Bless me with a miracle oh Lord! Everything you've promised me Lord, I pray you bring it to pass. Confirm my son ship in you Lord." I prayed so long that I ended up falling asleep. The next thing I knew, they were waking me up for dinner. I did not want to eat, so I slid my tray of food to a guy sitting next to me. After dinner, I went back to my cell and prayed some more. I did not come out for our free time. I just wanted to be alone and talk with the Lord. I fell asleep once more and in the wee hours of the night the guards came to my cell. They said, "Roll it up, you're going home." I had been in jail for forty-five days and now I was being released and did not know how, other than it was a miracle from God. I later found out that my pastor, Prince Davis, put some money together, bailed me out and paid my fines. Thus, they had to release me from jail. I couldn't get ahold of my mom or anyone to pick me up, so I took a cab to the church. When I walked in, the church was having service. Everyone was so excited to see me. One of my best friends, Minister Roi Ford, grabbed me and hugged me so hard, I felt like my ribs were going to break.

Soon after my release, I went to work at a lumber yard. It was the same lumber yard I worked at as a teenager, called Desert Lumber. I was working 12-16 hour shifts and though I was being blessed, my patience and my faith were constantly being tested. During the peak of the day hours, it would sometimes be well over 110 degrees outside, so most of the work had to be done around and after midnight. A couple of times I would get cussed out by one of the supervisors for no reason at all. I constantly asked God to strengthen me. I had never been very good at being cussed out and not doing anything about it. However, I constantly reminded myself that I was no longer the same as I used to be.

One night while I was at work, I needed a beam of lumber. So, I went to cut the wire that held all the beams together into one unit. When I cut the wire, all the beams fell on me. One beam had hit the top of my hand so hard that the bone looked as if it was sticking out of the bottom of my hand. The pain was excruciating, I knew it was broken. However, I didn't want to report this to my supervisor at the risk of becoming a liability on my much-needed job. I prayed to the Lord, and asked him to fix the situation and heal my hand, so I wouldn't lose my job. When I got home, I showed my mother and step father my hand. They both knew immediately that it was broken. My mother began to say, "Why didn't you go to the emergency room?!" She was a bit upset. As I began to explain why I didn't go, I told her God would fix it. She insisted that I go to the emergency room. I told her that if God didn't fix it by the morning I would let her take me to the ER, but I had to give God a chance first. I went to my room and prayed until I

54

fell asleep. I could not get comfortable, so I tossed and turned all night in great pain. Eventually I did fall asleep. I woke up and looked at the clock; it was 7:01 am and I realized I was laying on my broken hand. Afraid that I had made it worse by laying on it, I jumped up and looked at my hand. There wasn't a bruise and it wasn't broken; it wasn't even swollen. I ran back into my parents' room, woke them up and said, "Look what the Lord has done!" As a result, my parents never questioned God again. In fact, now, they are both in ministry until this very day. Now this is one of the many reasons I can say that God is real and he answers prayers.

Under the tutelage of Prince Davis I was able to find my place in ministry. I would preach in the church and on the street corners. I would also go into the juvenile hall facilities to speak to young gang members and to people who were like I was. While most of the time ministry was very satisfying to me, on many occasions after ministering to young people, I walked away feeling discouraged. It was as if my words of hope and encouragement would only fall on deaf ears. One night after speaking to a youth group in the juvenile hall facility, I left feeling discouraged; like I wasn't making a difference. So, I went to the church and laid at the altar. I prayed for a while, and then I fell asleep. I had a dream that I was a little skinny frail guy in the middle of a dry deserted place. I saw thousands of young people from a distance who stood from behind a gate and they were yelling, "Please help us! Please help us!" I began walking toward them and after every step I took, I grew bigger and stronger until eventually, as I got close to the gate, it was as if I was the Incredible Hulk. I had muscles everywhere with great strength. I ripped the gate open and I told the young people to follow me. Then I awoke from the dream. Immediately I knew what the meaning of this dream was. It had been a long time at this point since I had been in the gym lifting weights. Now, from that dream alone I knew that lifting weights and having muscles would play some part in this ministry.

So now my approach to the youth was much different. Not only did I speak the Gospel, but I was also able to incorporate weightlifting into my visits with the youth. I remember on one particular Sunday, I had preached and one kid came to the altar and broke down. He wanted to be saved, but he felt as if God wouldn't save him. We went to the back room, and I talked to him and shared scripture with him. I told him the same thing I told all the rest of the kids, that if God could save me he could save anybody but he still didn't believe me. He said that I was just a preacher with a suit and tie and could never understand the life he lived. I noticed his tattoos, which lead to me asking him, "What gang are you from?" Interestingly enough he said, "I'm from the Gerson Park Kingsman." I then asked him if he had ever heard of a guy named Madness from NTG. He said, "Oh sure, Madness died long ago." I said, "You're right, but Cory Mathews is still alive." He didn't understand, so he asked me what I meant. I took off my shirt and showed him the tattoos with the name "Madness." I told him that I was the guy whom they used to call Madness. I told him, "I have lived that same lifestyle and once again, if God has forgiven me, he can forgive you." That day he was baptized. This made me realize just how important my testimony was.

I then took my ministry and continued to preach on the street corners; however, this time I went to my old stomping grounds in the neighborhood I grew up in; The Regal Estates. Some of my old friends gathered around to hear me preach, one of whom was one of my childhood friends named Gavin, whom we called G Stone. After the message, I asked him to come for prayer, and said now was the time to give his life to Jesus. With watery eyes, he said he wasn't ready yet. One week from that day, my friend, Gavin, was gunned down and killed. Months later during a Wednesday Bible study, Bushwick's younger brother, Glen Taylor, came to the church. He wanted to talk to me outside. For some reason, he appeared to be upset which was not normal for him. I watched him grow up and knew he was a hustler and down for the set. After we talked he said that he was going to come back to church on Sunday but for now, he had to go. As Sunday morning came around, Glen never showed, but on Mondays the church doors would be open for noon day Bible study and prayer. While we were having prayer, an old friend of mine, Coretta, whom we also called "Girly" came running into the church hysterically screaming, "Cory! Cory! Baby Glen is dead! Can you please come to the house and pray for us? You're the only person the family would hear." So, Sister Jerri Coleman and myself left the church and went to pray for the family. We found out that he had been killed at a car show.

CHAPTER 13

By now, five years had passed since my being in ministry, and with that, there was also five years of celibacy. I hadn't even dated a woman in that time. Some days I would find myself very lonely. I had begun to remind God of the blessing he laid on my heart when I gave my life to him and the dream I had about him giving me the best things I could ever ask for which in my mind, once again, I knew it was about being loved and having my own family. It was hard sometimes because the ministers and all my friends would often go to dinner and movies with their spouses, yet I was single. Looking back I now realize how important that time in my life was. I was able to be exclusively God's. My mother would often make comments about how she wanted grandchildren and my sister even wanted me to have a girlfriend. Though I longed for a woman's companionship, the Lord blessed me and I was surrounded by loving church mothers. They prayed for me daily and always made sure I had good home cooked meals. They loved me as if I was their own child. In so many ways, I can say they set a very high standard for any woman that was going to be in my life.

I was 28 years old by now. My sister and one of my best friends, Roi Ford, with his wife, Shanti, came to me and asked if I would mind dating a younger woman. I asked who they had in mind. Of course, for me, if it was God's will, it was all good. They asked me how I felt about one of the young sisters in the church whose name was Lori. I always thought she was beautiful. Nonetheless, I always figured she was just too young. I watched her grow up over the past four years in the church. I remember when she was baptized, she was about 15 years old, and she was a blessing in the youth ministry. Now she was 18 years old. She was very mature beyond her years. Just like myself she didn't talk much, but we all went out one night to a Japanese restaurant called Osaka. It was probably the most fun I'd had in a very long time. We were both able to relax and enjoy our night, with our friends.

During those days, we'd hang out and she'd make me tea just the way I liked it. I knew she was special because being around her, I was able to laugh and smile. I even learned how to joke a little bit and have a good time. Being youthful was unfamiliar territory, mainly due to my past. However, when I was with her, I felt that one piece of life that was missing for so long. Many people were in disagreement with me about my relationship with Lori, mainly because of our age difference. However, that never changed the fact that I knew there was something special about her. Eventually, months had past. I was having a rough day at work one day, and my pastor called. He said. "Hey son, you have a minute?" I said yes. He said, "This may come as a shock to you." He then asked me if I loved Lori. I replied, "Yes, sir. I have to be honest, I do love her." He said. "Ok, marry her." Now, at this time in my life he was probably the only person in the whole world that had a very big influence on me, mainly because he was like my dad, and because I respected and admired his walk with Jesus. So, I knew that him saying, "Marry Lori" was as good as God speaking. He then went on to tell me how God dealt with his heart about me being married to Lori. He added and said, "Look, don't worry about what anyone says. And don't worry about anyone else's feelings. This right here is the Lord's way." That's all I needed to hear.

So, a few days later after Bible study one night, Lori and I went to grab a bite to eat. Being so late, Denny's was the only place open. We sat there talking and eating, and in the most unromantic way, I looked at her and casually said, "You wanna marry me?" I guess it must of took her by surprise because she just looked at me kind of strange. Then she said, "Really?! Are you serious?!" I replied, "Yes! Will you marry me?" With a big smile on her face, she said yes. Lori and I were young, in love and on fire for the Lord. We set a date for our wedding, but unfortunately, four weeks prior to the date of the wedding, Lori's mother passed away from cancer. All I knew was that I had to be strong for her and be there for her family. Lori was very strong herself though. She insisted that we continue our wedding plans. So, on July 15, 2006, we got married, and we are still and even more madly in love to this day.

About a few months after our wedding date, my wife found out she was pregnant with our first child. On April 13, 2007, my little princess was born. I named her Rhema, because it was during a time in my life when God was speaking so expressly to me. No matter how big or how tough I seemed to be, when my daughter was born and I was able to hold her, I melted. I was just a big ole teddy bear. She definitely had me wrapped around her little finger. Two months later, as the Lord would have it, my pastor was in Dallas, Texas. He had started a ministry, in the Dallas area. It had been going strong now for about a year. He called me one day and asked me if I would be able to fly down and minister at their church. I said to him, "Anytime, I could come this next weekend." I had been down there several times to preach before. I assumed he was talking about just coming down for a weekend to preach but then he replied, "No, when can you move down here, and pastor this church?" I said, "I will put my two week notice in at my job," for God had already moved on my heart. So, weeks later, my wife, two-month-old daughter and I packed up all we could into our little minivan and moved to Dallas, Texas. It was a huge leap of faith for me. I had to trust God on a whole new Level. As soon as we moved out to Texas, my wife was pregnant again, now with our second baby.

CHAPTER 14

This part of my life was very challenging. My wife and I were still practically newlyweds, only being married for a little over a year. We had a newborn baby, Lori was pregnant with our second and we lived in a city where we didn't know anyone, except the few people in our ministry. That being said, times were scary. We lived in a very poor part of North Arlington in a rundown apartment complex. A drug dealer lived right next door, and a pimp and prostitute lived right upstairs. Every night we'd hear the pimp beating his woman, and the police constantly were on the property. There were drug addicts and drug activity going on all through the night in front of our apartment. I hated my wife feeling uncomfortable, and I vowed within myself to put my family in a better position.

Our church was very small; however, we committed ourselves to doing God's work, believing that God had us here for a reason. It was a while before I had my first job in Texas. During that time, we were totally dependent upon God to miraculously provide. There were times where it seemed as if we were drowning in poverty. We didn't know where our next meal would come from. However, when we look back at those times, we can see God never let us down. My wife and I would constantly pray together, and we remained faithful in ministry and to one another. God consistently answered our prayers. We'd get calls from people all over the country saying that God had placed us on their hearts, and people wanted to be a blessing to us. People began to pour in. I witnessed to people every opportunity I found, inviting people to church. During the day, I'd constantly look for jobs and during the night we'd have prayer meetings and Bible study. God provided finances in mysterious ways. I look back now, and I realize just how good God is, and that he never let us down. We were very blessed.

Jobs would not hire me because of my felony convictions, so I called Lawrence Weekly in Las Vegas and asked if he could maybe write me a letter of reference, or if he knew anyone that could help me get a job. Of course, my passion was ministry but I loved dealing with youth, gang members particularly. So, I was able to land a job with a youth program called T Cap. It was a youth program that dealt with at risk and troubled youth. We partnered with the parole and probation department. I was given the opportunity to go back into the facilities and do gang intervention and ministry. I loved that job. However, it didn't pay the bills. So, I needed a bit more income with my second baby on the way. I started training at Gold's Gym in North Arlington. I'd often go there at night to work out by myself. One night while I was working out, I noticed a guy laying on the bench unconscious. His skin was purple, so I ran to him immediately. He had a barbell with 275 pounds of weight laying against his throat and his arms were dangling. I took the barbell off his throat and felt for a pulse; he had none. I screamed at the top of my lungs for someone to help and call an ambulance. Though he didn't have a pulse his body was still very warm, so I began to whisper to him, "It's not your time to go. Don't die." I began praying as hard as I could and the man started convulsing as if he was going into a seizure. So, I wrapped him in my arms and laid him down on his side, eagerly waiting for the medics to arrive. Finally, they did, and as the man came back to consciousness, they took him to the hospital. It just so happened that while he was bench pressing, his arm broke in three different places and the weight fell on his neck, cutting off his circulation. I was very thankful to God that he survived.

Days later I went back to the gym to work out and I was approached by the owner. He wanted to personally thank me for saving that man's life. He asked me if there was anything he could do to show his appreciation. I said, "If you can hire me, I'll be the best employee you ever had". He said, "Do you have any experience training people?" I told him I didn't have my certification, but I had plenty experience. He said, "You're hired." I was also contacted by the man who survived the whole incident. He wanted to take me out to dinner and say thank you. So, he did, and said, "If I had a million dollars right now, I'd give it to you. I wish I could pay you back for saving my life." I replied, "You don't have to pay me anything, but how about this? It was God who saved you; I just so happened to be there. So, if you want to thank anyone, come and fellowship with me at my church. That would be reward enough for me." He said, "Is that all? When is the next service?" Shortly after, he joined our church.

Just a couple of weeks later, our second child was born; a son! With everything that had gone on in the past year and all the changes we had gone through, I called my son Elijah. He was such a beautiful baby, and just like Elijah in the Bible, he was a hairy little fella. My heart was so full of joy, and once again, I was but a big ole teddy bear. With my new family, I could tell that God was yet answering prayers. However, times would continue to be very challenging. I received a phone call from home in Las Vegas and I was told that Bushwick had gotten killed. He was gunned down in the wee hours of the night. My heart dropped. I screamed at the top of my lungs and cried. Until this very day, I sure do miss him. Though with much prayer and comforting words from my family, I was able to overcome my hour of grief. And so, I did. I continued to work hard and provide for my family at my new job.

Working at Gold's Gym was an experience all in its own. I was able to train in a very competitive atmosphere. I was also blessed to meet big people in the bodybuilding industry. It was there that I met Gus Carter and Ronnie Coleman. We started to work out together. Eventually, we took our training to Ronnie's home gym, Metroflex, which was a hardcore dungeon-type gym where all the top competitors in Texas would go train. This is also where I met a man by the name of Brian Dobson, who is the owner of Metroflex Gym, the guy responsible for discovering Ronnie Coleman and who had trained many champions. My life was constantly changing, in a good way of course. My wife was expecting our third child, the ministry was working pretty well and we had a few new friends who turned out to be big supporters later in my bodybuilding career. About two months later, my wife and I welcomed our third child to the world; another son whom we named Isaiah Cory. You would think by now I was used to this experience, but each time witnessing each child take their first breath, I would melt inside.

Soon after, Ronnie mentioned that I should compete in his show, the Ronnie Coleman Classic. I remember my exact thoughts were, "I'm just a small guy. I only weigh 212 pounds. How could I possibly compete against those monsters?" So, I responded to him and said, "Really?!" He said, "Yeah! You're big and you can beat everybody out there." Gus said the exact same thing, but since it would be my first show, Gus suggested that I should compete at the Lone Star Classic, which was about nine weeks away. I learned from them as much as I could; what to eat and how to train. However, a week before the show I was very timid and nervous because I didn't know how to pose. Gus only cared about training and Ronnie was out of town quite a bit, so a friend set me up with a lady named Terri Harris. She was a bodybuilder and a posing coach. Terri dropped by the next day for my first posing practice. She was like a drill sergeant. She taught me how to pose within that week. She also became very close friends with my wife and me. She would come by to spend time with the kids.

So finally, the day of my first show came. I took first place in my division and also won the overall. My wife, Terri, Gus, Ronnie and close friends Ben Holt and Wes Smith were all so excited. We immediately began to talk about what my second show would be. Being six weeks away, I was now set to do the Europa which was a much bigger and more competitive stage. So, I trained and prepared myself to compete on the next level. When the show came, I placed third. Everyone was so excited because third place was still a huge accomplishment. However, I was very disappointed. I am very competitive, so I didn't want to lose to anyone. I agreed to prepare for the next show which was the Ronnie Coleman Classic.

The Ronnie Coleman Classic was an even bigger show than the Europa. It would be my third show, and only the best in the state of Texas would compete on this stage. This was also the time in which the Gold's Gym I worked at was closing down. Without work, made my contest preparation became very difficult. In addition to that, my wife was now pregnant with our fourth child. So now with three children and a wife to support with a baby on the way, I had no real means of finances. My wife and I would spend many hours in prayer until one day, my friend, Ben Holt, who was a vice president of a company, offered me a job. So, I began working at his warehouse. I wasn't making much, but at least it was enough to sustain my family and me. Ronnie would take money out of his own pocket to make sure I had everything I needed so I could continue training. Finally, when the time came for the Ronnie Coleman Classic, the guy who beat me at the Europa and many other great competitors lined up next to me on that stage, but I was determined to win. And so, I did. I won first in light heavyweight and overall.

Conversations quickly arose concerning my next competition, which would be the 2011 Nationals held in Miami Beach. The Nationals were considered to be one of the biggest, if not the biggest amateur show in the nation. This show also would determine what amateur bodybuilder would go on to become professional and earn pro status. Weeks before the Nationals, my wife was nearly due to give birth any day and though I was working in this little warehouse, I did not have the financial means to continue to prepare for the Nationals. That's when Brian Dobson bought my plane ticket, and another friend by the name of Joe Lobell put $900 in my pocket and insisted that I continue training and preparing for the show. And so, I did. On September 2nd, our fourth child was born and we named him Joshua Caleb. My son, just like all the others, turned me into a teddy bear. When it came time for the show, Terri Harris accompanied me to Miami to help with the final stages of contest prep, helping me to be the best that I could be. I placed fourth among forty or so competitors in my class.

CHAPTER 15

Finishing fourth place was considered very impres̲.̲v̲c̲, being that it was my first time competing on a national stage. When I had gotten back home, the warehouse I was working at laid everyone off. So again, I had no job. However, I did have a dream. Fourth place on the biggest stage only meant that I could get better. I was just within grasp of becoming a professional bodybuilder. Being without a job, Brian Dobson allowed me to come into the gym and become a full-time personal trainer. My vehicle had broken down beyond repair so I was without transportation, but Brian bought me a minivan so I could continue training people and prepare for what would be my next big show, which was the USA in Las Vegas. I continued to train and make improvements to my physique. This time at the USA, I placed third. I received so much encouragement from my friends, family members and fans. People like Brian Dobson and Ronnie Coleman continued to support me, in hopes that I pursue my endeavors to become a professional bodybuilder. So now my next show was in 2012, again at the Nationals, this time held in Atlanta, Georgia. Everything seemed to come together, just in time for me to step on the biggest stage in the nation once again. I had so much fun at the Nationals in Atlanta. This time at this show, I earned my pro card, becoming a professional bodybuilder. I had an overwhelming response from so many people, most of whom I've never met. Everyone was so excited, but I just wanted to go home and be with my family.

Something that up until now had seemed so vague, had now become a reality. I was actually a professional bodybuilder! This was like one in a thousand! When I got to the airport to go back to Texas, I was surrounded by people wanting pictures and autographs. I knew that my life had changed. Once I got home, my wife and children had cookies, cakes, and pizza with balloons and banners. We celebrated. Even the church celebrated. Everyone gathered over to the house to share this moment with me. Not long after, I signed a contract to become one of Ronnie Coleman's VIP Athletes, and I would go on to compete in my first pro show, the Dallas Europa. However, just one week before The Europa, I received a phone call saying that my very close friend, Terri Harris, had passed away. This weighed very heavy on me, even to the point of being depressed and questioning my continuing to compete. After talking with Ronnie, he encouraged me to get back in the gym and finish training for this show. So, I did. My motivation became to accomplish what Terri always told me could be accomplished, as she was always one of the few who believed in me becoming pro. So, I went on to compete and placed an amazing fifth place at the Dallas Europa. I was overcome with every emotion you could think of. Dedicating my placing to her, I found comfort in knowing that she would have been beyond proud.

Even though it was just fifth place, I got lots of publicity and many doors began to open as a result. Now that I was competing professionally, I went on to compete in various shows, climbing the ranks amongst the best in the world. Looking back over my life, I realize just how God had orchestrated things. God had placed specific people in my life, Ronnie Coleman being among them. He was an answer to many prayers. We had, over the years, become just like brothers. There were times where we would go to the grocery store and Ronnie would fill the grocery cart full of meat, just for me to have food for my contest prep. And now, looking at where I am as a professional bodybuilder and one of his athletes, I see my life was quickly heading in an upward direction. I continued to train for shows and compete. Eventually, a good friend of mine and Brian Dobson's, who was a pastor of a church, would come to the gym regularly to train with me. Needless to say, this was also a blessing. We'd support each other's ministry, until one day God laid upon my heart to merge ministries. And so, we did. My wife and I, and the members of my church, began attending service with Jonathan String fellow at Rock Church Arlington. God was blessing us in so many ways. My family was being blessed, and other opportunities and endorsements presented themselves.

In addition to being a Ronnie Coleman athlete, I was also a Gorilla Wear sponsored athlete. I had come a long way from being a gangster, a drug addict and a pimp. Now, traveling all over the world, and having so many great fans and so many great friends, I can say my life is beyond blessed. My children are my biggest fans. God even restored my relationship with my first-born son, C'Tory Mathews. I continue to speak to youth and remain an ambassador for Christ. The struggle that I once knew has become my greatest strength.

AT THIS CHAPTER IN MY LIFE, I HAVE CLOSED MY TROPHY CASE FROM BODYBUILDING AND HAVE RETIRED, IN EXCHANGE TO BECOME A TROPHY FOR GOD.

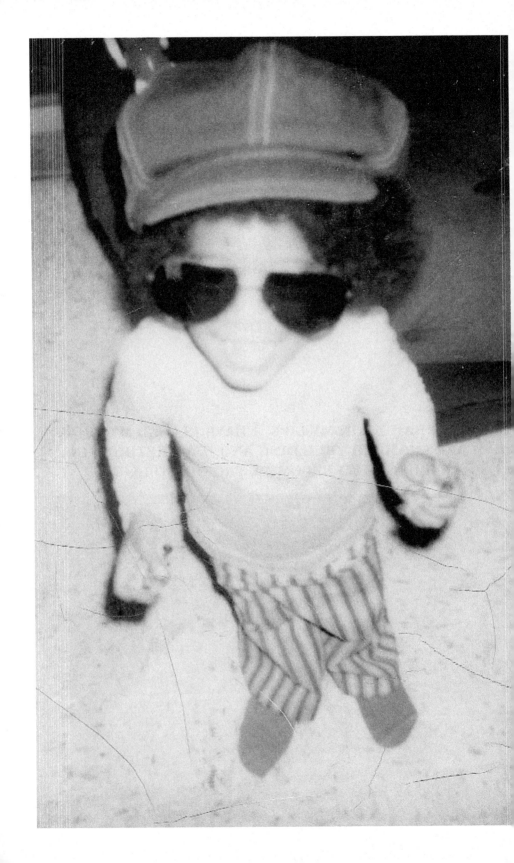

In Precious Memory
of
Michael Darnell McCraney

July 27, 1975   March 23, 1992

*But when Jesus saw it, He was much displeased, and saith
unto them, suffer the little children to come unto me,
and forbid them not: for of such is the kingdom of God.*

St. Mark 10:14

SERVICES
Saturday, March 28, 1992
2:00 p.m.

Palm Mortuary
1325 North Main Street
Las Vegas, Nevada 89101

OFFICIANT
Rev. A. J. Thompson
Victory Baptist Church

In Loving Memory

of

Gerald Lamont Johnson

June 14, 1975   *August 1, 1992*

SERVICES
Thursday, August 6, 1992
1:00 p.m.

West Las Vegas Memorial Chapel
615 W. Van Buren Avenue
Las Vegas, Nevada

INTERMENT
Woodlawn Cemetery
Las Vegas, Nevada

In Precious Memory

of

ISAAC TORRIE BETHEA MARABLE

November 3, 1975   *May 29, 1993*

SERVICES
Thursday, June 3, 1993
1:00 P.M.

ST. JOHN CHURCH OF GOD IN CHRIST
2301 Comstock Drive
North Las Vegas, Nevada
Elder O.L. Jefferson, Pastor

OFFICIANT
Minister Isaac Bethea

IN LOVING MEMORY
OF
JOHN LEE DAVIS

Sunrise
May 8, 1970

Sunset
October 4, 1996

SERVICES
SATURDAY, OCTOBER 12, 1996
11:00 A.M.

℘

HOLY GHOST TEMPLE
2624 CLAYTON AVENUE
LAS VEGAS, NV 89110

OFFICIATING
PASTOR LEONARD JOHNSON

Homegoing Celebration
for
Anthony R. Glenn (Drumgole)

Sunrise
November 26, 1962

Sunset
June 15, 1998

Services
Saturday, June 20, 1998
1:00 P.M.

True Love Baptist Church
1941 H Street
The Rev. I. W. Wilson, Pastor

SERVICE ENTRUSTED TO:
AMERICAN BURIAL & CREMATION SERVICES
310 Foremaster Lane
Las Vegas, Nevada 89101

Celebrating The Homecoming

Of

GLENN CHARLES TAYLOR JR.
"B.G."

Sunrise: June 7, 1978   **Sunset: October 10, 2004**

Service

Tuesday, October 19, 2004 at 11:00 a.m.
Full Gossip Church
817 Carey Street
Las Vegas, NV 89030

Officiant

Reverend Flack, Pastor
Full Gossip Church

Homecoming Celebration

Of

James Marlow Gipson - Andrews

Sunrise: October 22, 1981   Sunset: August 26, 2007

Service

Saturday, September 8th, 2007 at 12:00 p.m.
Bunkers Funeral Home
925 Las Vegas Blvd 89101
Hosting Minister
Pastor Mike Hatch
1316 Miller Ave
Las Vegas, Nevada 89030

A Celebration of an Extraordinary Life

for

Katherine Kay (Kat)

Sunrise
December 4, 1958

Sunset
December 16, 2010

Service
Monday, December 27, 2010
11:00 a.m.

Tried Stone Baptist Church
621 W. Carey Ave.
North Las Vegas, NV 89030

Officiant: Reverend Ronnie Smith, Pastor

From Earth to Serenity

Coretta

"GIRLY" YOLANDA TAYLOR

JOYFUL   SADNESS
FEBUARY 7, 1969   JANUARY 20, 2016

SATURDAY, JANUARY 30, 2016
11:00AM

GOD'S HOUSE INTERNATIONAL
1072 W. BARTLETT AVE. | LAS VEGAS, NV 89106
BISHOP ADAM ADDISON, OFFICIATING

Other Great Titles....

Hard Questions About

Angels & Demons

International Bestseller

By Only A. Guy

Most every Christian has questions they don't know quite know how to answer to unbelievers or even other Christians. This book covers the hard questions about Angles and Demons, with plain answers. Such questions as:

What does the Bible say about angels?
What does the Bible say about demons?
Are demons fallen angels?
What do angels look like?
Can Satan read our minds/know our thoughts?

The answers within this book will help guide you toward a stronger faith and a hunger for God's Word. Remember a closed mind can't get fed.

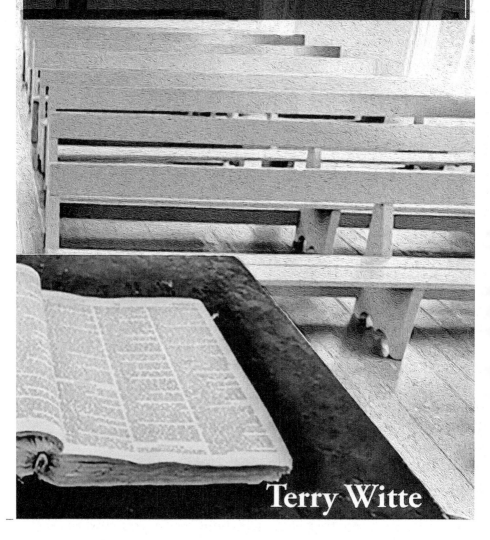

So You Think God Has Called You to Be a Pastor:
What Pastors, Pastors -To-Be,
Elders or Anyone in a
Congregation Should Look for
in The Leadership of their Church

Terry Witte

God, for whatever reason, has graciously involved me in a number of different ministries during my Christian walk. I experienced many church-related situations where I didn't truly understand or recognize why things were the way they were. Unfortunately, I have seen some of those in leadership position fail for one reason or another and I ask myself "why would educated, well-meaning, Christian men leave the ministry or why doesn't their church grow?" After many years of being involved in various ministries, I have come up with the conclusion that it does not have to be the case.

It appears to me that most of the time when things don't work out, it all goes back to the leadership's ability to make good biblical decisions concerning the church and their role in it. I wrote this book in hopes that it could be used as a positive tool for anyone in leadership to evaluate their own walk and possibly even help those fellow leaders who may be struggling in their efforts to fulfill their calling. It is also a possible type of resource for a new, or a pastor-to-be, made aware of some of the pitfalls Satan has used to destroy other pastors and churches that have gone before them. Over the years I have been asked by various Christians as to what they should be looking for in a biblically-based church? This book will help them evaluate which church they might want to become a member of.

I don't claim to have all the answers to the many problems the church faces in today's dark world. I do want to pass on some possible ways to avoid and handle some of the everyday challenges those who minister in it will be faced with, things I wish I knew before I started to actively serve in leadership. This book is filled with true life stories of how God has worked in my life to refine and guide me so I could be of help to others in like situations to survive the spiritual battle we are all in.

Hard Questions About

Salvation

International Bestseller

By Only A. Guy

Every Christian has questions they don't know quite how to answer to believers and unbelivers alike. This book covers the hard questions about salvation, with plain answers. Such questions as:

What happens to those who have never heard about Jesus?
What happened to those who believed in God before Jesus?
Why is Christianity such a bloody religion?
What does it mean to be a born again Christian?

The answers within this book will help guide you toward a stronger faith and a hunger for God's Word. Remember a closed mind can't get fed.

CPSIA information can be obtained
at www.ICGtesting.com
Printed in the USA
BVOW06s2048220617
487627BV00003B/4/P